Trading Away from Conflict

DIRECTIONS IN DEVELOPMENT
Trade

Trading Away from Conflict

Using Trade to Increase Resilience in Fragile States

Massimiliano Calì

WORLD BANK GROUP

Library of Congress Cataloging-in-Publication Data

Calì, Massimiliano.
Trading away from conflict : using trade to increase resilience in fragile states / Massimiliano Calì.
  pages cm. — (Directions in development)
  Includes bibliographical references.
ISBN 978-1-4648-0308-6 (alk. paper) — ISBN 978-1-4648-0309-3 (ebk)
  1. Developing countries—Commercial policy. 2. Developing countries—Commerce—Political aspects. 3. Insurgency—Economic aspects—Developing countries. 4. Economic development—Political aspects—Developing countries. I. World Bank. II. Title.
  HF1413.C355 2014
  382'.3091724—dc23
                                                                                2014030078

Contents

Acknowledgments   *ix*
About the Author   *xi*
Abbreviations   *xiii*

Overview   1
Introduction   1
Main Results   2
Policy Directions   4
Notes   6
References   7

Chapter 1   **How Trade Can Affect Conflict**   9
Introduction   9
Trade Flows in Fragile Countries Are Different   12
Why Changes in Trade Flows May Affect Conflict   18
Cross-Country Evidence on Trade Shocks and Conflict   25
Evidence from Nigerian States (2004–13)   34
Evidence from the Israeli-Palestinian Conflict (2000–04)   42
Notes   51
References   54

Chapter 2   **Conditions That Affect the Impact of Trade Shocks
             on Conflict**   59
Introduction   59
Grievances   61
Institutional Capacity and Inclusiveness   63
Conditions in Neighboring Countries   65
Transmission of Prices to Domestic Markets   65
Cross-Country Empirical Tests   66
Testing for the Importance of Heterogeneity in
    the Nigerian Conflict   72
Heterogeneity in the Israeli-Palestinian Conflict   73
Notes   73
References   75

Chapter 3   How Trade Policy Could Ease Tensions in
             Fragile Countries   79
             Trade Policies in Fragile Countries Must Take into
                Account the Implications for Conflict   80
             Manage Receipts from Commodity Exports in a
                Conflict-Sensitive Way   81
             Protect Producers, Consumers, and Workers from Adverse
                Trade Shocks   85
             Promote Trade with Neighbors   86
             Support Labor-Intensive Exports   86
             Build Long-Term Conflict Resilience   87
             Notes   88
             References   89

Appendix A   Data Issues   93

Appendix B   Estimation Methodology and Empirical Results   109

Boxes

1.1   Which Are the Fragile Countries?   12
1.2   Empirical Issues in the Early Literature on the Relationship
       between Changes in Income and Conflict   26
1.3   The South Sudanese Civil War: Was Oil Export the Trigger?   28
1.4   Correcting for Endogeneity When Measuring the Relationship
       between Conflict and Trade under RTAs   30
1.5   The Literature on the Israeli-Palestinian Conflict and
       the Opportunity Cost of Violence   43

Figures

O.1   Most of the Poor Will Soon Be in Fragile Countries   2
1.1   Trade Represents the Major Source of Foreign Exchange in
       Fragile States   13
1.2   Share of Largest Exports in Selected Fragile Countries and
       Territories (in 2010)   14
1.3   For Many Fragile States, Exports Are Not Heavily Diversified   15
1.4   For Fragile States, Net Food Imports Constitute a Higher
       Percentage of GDP   16
1.5   Fragile Countries Perform Worse Than Their Peers in Trade
       Facilitation and the Gap Is Growing   17
1.6   Mapping the Linkages between Changes in Trade Flows and
       Civil Conflict   19
1.7   Palestinian Exports to the World and to Israel, 1996–2000   44
1.8   Distribution of Changes in Palestinian Exports (1996–99)   45
1.9   Palestinians Killed by Israel in the West Bank and Gaza, 2000–04   46

1.10   Israeli Imports from China and the West Bank and Gaza,
        1995–2000   49
2.1   Marginal Effects of Px Across the Range of Interaction
        Variables' Values   70
B.1   Changes in Israeli MFN Tariffs (5-digit SITC Rev. 3), 1993–2004   127

Maps
1.1   The Geography of Conflict in Nigeria (2004–13)   36
1.2   Conflict Intensity across States in Nigeria   36
1.3   Violence Intensity across States in Nigeria   37

Tables
1.1   Fragile Countries' Exports Are Less Diversified Than Other
        Developing Countries' Exports   14
1.2   Classification of the Export Commodities (with Example)   21
2.1   Under What Conditions Are the Marginal Effects of Trade
        Shocks Not Significant?   69
2.2   Lebanon Has a Higher Risk of Conflict from Hydrocarbons
        Exports than the Average Country   71
A.1   Fragile Countries and Territories and Number of Battle Deaths   93
A.2   Summary Statistics, Cross-Country Analysis   97
A.3   Interaction Variables for the Cross-Country Analysis   97
A.4   Household Per Capita Expenditure on Food and
        Nonfood by Zone   101
A.5   Summary Statistics of the Regressors (2004–11)   101
A.6   Summary Statistics for Key Variables in the Israeli-Palestinian
        Conflict Study   103
A.7   Description of Variables Used in the Palestinian Case Study   104
B.1   The Impact of Trade on Conflict, Cross-Country Analysis   112
B.2   Robustness with Fast-Moving, Country-Specific Time Trends,
        Cross-Country Analysis   113
B.3   Robustness for Price Makers and Conflict Data Source,
        Cross-Country Analysis   113
B.4   Splitting the Commodities' Variables into Different Types,
        Cross-Country Analysis   114
B.5   The Impact of Trade Variables on the Likelihood of Conflict
        Coming to an End, Cross-Country Analysis   115
B.6   The Impact of Trade on Battle Deaths, Cross-Country Analysis   116
B.7   The Effect of Trading with Neighbors on Conflict, Revisited,
        Cross-Country Analysis   117
B.8   Trade Variables without Lag Structure, Cross-Country Analysis   118
B.9   Summary Statistics of the Dependent Variable (2004–11),
        Nigeria   119

B.10   The Impact of Price Shocks on Conflict Events in Nigeria
        (2004–11)   121
B.11   The Impact of Price Shocks on Conflict in Nigeria (2004–11),
        Robustness   122
B.12   The Impact of Price Shocks on Various Types of Conflict in
        Nigeria (2004–11)   123
B.13   Mediating Factors Affecting the Impact of Price Shocks on
        Conflict   124
B.14   The Impact of Changes in Trade Prices on the Boko Haram
        Conflict (2010–13)   125
B.15   The Impact of Palestinian Exports on Conflict Intensity   129
B.16   The Impact of Palestinian Trade on Conflict Intensity   130
B.17   The Impact of Palestinian Trade on a Different Measure of
        Conflict Intensity   131
B.18   The Impact of Palestinian Trade on Conflict Probability   131
B.19   The Impact of Palestinian Trade on Conflict: Tackling
        Endogeneity   132
B.20   The Heterogeneity of the Impact of Export Changes on
        Conflict Intensity   132
B.21   Instrumenting Palestinian Exports through Exogenous Shocks   133

Acknowledgments

This report was prepared by Massimiliano Calì, Trade Economist (Trade and Competitiveness Global Practice), on the basis of studies conducted together with a team of consultants comprising Babatunde Abidoye (University of Pretoria), Amir Fouad (Consultant, Trade and Competitiveness Global Practice), Sami Miaari (Tel Aviv University), and Alen Mulabdic (Graduate Institute of International Studies). William Shaw (Consultant, Trade and Competitiveness Global Practice) helped put together the report.

The report benefited considerably from the overall guidance and comments provided by Mona Haddad, Practice Manager (Trade and Competitiveness Global Practice). Peer reviewers Quy-Toan Do, Senior Economist (Development Research Group), and Raju Singh, Lead Economist (Macroeconomics and Fiscal Management Global Practice), provided excellent comments that considerably improved the report. Marie Yenko provided able editorial assistance.

Useful comments were also provided at various stages of the project by Nicolas Berman, Elena Ianchovichina, Philip Keefer, Charles Kunaka, Eric Le Borgne, Daniel Lederman, Hani Mansour, Renzo Massari, Gary Milante, Nadia Piffaretti, Nicola Pontara, Espen Prydz, Nadia Selim, Radhika Srinivasan, and Yongmei Zhou.

This project was supported in part by the governments of Finland, Norway, Sweden, and the United Kingdom through the Multi-Donor Trust Fund for Trade and Development.

About the Author

Massimiliano Calì is a trade economist at the World Bank. His current and recent work focuses on the relation between economics and conflict, on the poverty impact of trade, and on migration. Prior to joining the Bank in 2012, he served as an economic advisor to the Palestinian Ministry of National Economy in Ramallah, as a research fellow with the Overseas Development Institute, and as an economist with the Italian Embassy to Bolivia. In these capacities he has provided economic policy advice to a number of Ministries in developing countries as well as to international organizations and NGOs. His work has been published in academic journals, books, and official reports. He holds a PhD in economic geography from the London School of Economics, an MA in development economics from the University of East Anglia, and a BA in economics from the University of Pavia.

Abbreviations

ACLED	Armed Conflict Location and Events Dataset
AGOA	Africa Growth and Opportunity Act
CASA	Conflict Affected States in Africa
COW	Correlates of War Project
CPIA	country policy and institutional assessment
DDPs	direct dividend payments
EITI	extractive industries transparency initiative
FCS	Fragile and Conflict-Affected Situations
FDI	foreign direct investment
FSI	Failed States Index
GFRP	Global Food Crisis Response Program
KP	Kimberley Process
LPI	logistics performance indicator
MFN	Most Favoured Nation
NBS	National Bureau of Statistics
NTMs	nontariff measures
ODA	official development assistance
PLFS	Palestinian Labor Force Survey
PWYP	publish what you pay
RTAs	regional trade agreements
SWF	Sovereign Wealth Fund
ZINB	zero-inflated negative binomial estimator

Overview

Introduction

In the past 30 years the world has become much less poor everywhere except in fragile countries. By 2015 most of the world's poor are expected to live in fragile countries (figure O.1).[1] The majority of these countries has been, or still is, affected by civil conflicts. In addition to exacting a huge toll on human life, civil conflicts cause protracted, severe disruption of economic activities and infrastructure, and are key constraints to development in many countries. Cognizant of these challenges, the International Development Association (IDA) has provided over $11.2 billion in post-conflict reconstruction assistance to "fragile and conflict affected situations" since 2000.[2] However, the challenges in these countries remain daunting.

Fragile and conflict-affected countries are not only home to an increasing share of the world's poor; they are also at a greater risk of relapsing into conflict than other countries. Nearly 90 percent of the conflicts between 2000 and 2010 occurred in countries that had already experienced a recent conflict; almost half of the post-conflict countries relapse into conflict within 10 years (World Bank 2011a). Republic of South Sudan and the Central African Republic are but the latest examples of fragile countries that fell back into conflict. The challenge is particularly daunting in sub-Saharan Africa, where most countries at risk of conflict are concentrated.[3]

Trade and trade policy can greatly affect the risk of conflict. Trade encourages the reallocation of resources to more efficient activities, and thus opens up opportunities and creates jobs. However, changes in relative prices as a result of trade can also destroy opportunities and jobs in declining sectors, and the people affected by these losses may, under certain conditions, turn to violence as a source of income. Changes in real incomes generated by trade are particularly important in fragile states, where trade flows tend to be larger and more volatile than other external flows, such as aid, remittances and foreign investment. This volatility is partly due to these countries' low diversification and their high dependence on primary export commodities, which may exacerbate the effects of abrupt changes in exports on conflict. For example, a sharp fall in international coffee prices in Colombia during the 1990s lowered wages and increased violence more in coffee-producing municipalities than in other municipalities

Figure O.1 Most of the Poor Will Soon Be in Fragile Countries

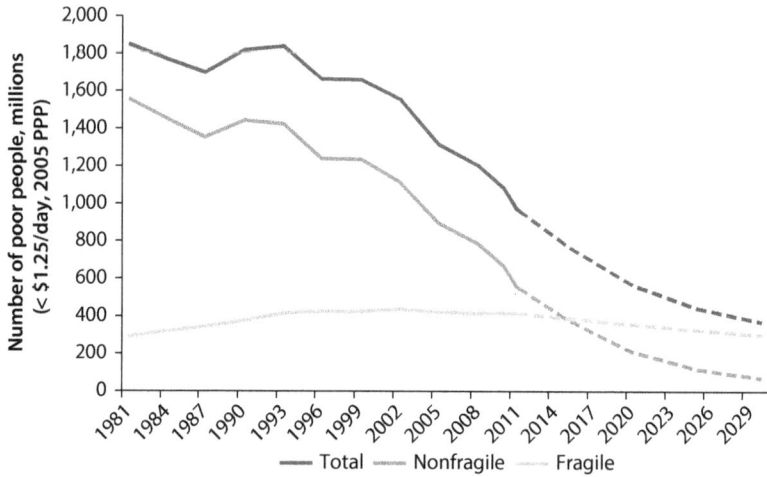

Sources: Historic (1981–2011) data from PovcalNet (accessed Oct. 10, 2014). Projections based on 10-year historic growth scenario from Lakner, Negre, and Prydz (2014).
Note: Estimates from counties on the OECD Fragile States list from 2014. Poverty estimates only from countries where at least one houshold survey and PPP conversion factors available. For 18 countries of the 51 on the list, we do not have such data. These missing countries comprise about 10 percent of the total population in fragile states.

(Dube and Vargas 2013). In addition, the majority of fragile countries are net food importers, so they are particularly exposed to the recent swings in international food prices. A number of governments in the Middle East and North Africa responded to the social unrest at the onset of the Arab Spring by extending food and fuel subsidies (World Bank 2011b). Countries also may be exposed to changes in the international demand for their products due to changes in their trading partners' incomes or changes in the access to foreign markets.

This report aims to understand how changes in imports and exports affect the risk and intensity of conflict and to help policy makers use trade to reduce this risk. In this way, it attempts to explicitly incorporate a fragility lens into the standard trade policy discussion in fragile countries. In doing so, the report also makes a number of contributions to the nascent but growing empirical literature on the relationship between changes in trade and conflict. It uses three different sets of data to do so: the experience of conflict across countries from 1960 to 2010, conflict across states in Nigeria from 2004 to 2013, and conflict during the Second Intifada in the West Bank and Gaza from September 2000 to December 2004.

Main Results

The analysis considers three main mechanisms for how trade-related changes can affect conflict. The opportunity cost effect holds that changes in real incomes, for example driven by changes in trade prices, change incentives for participating in conflict by changing the return on participation in violence compared with more productive activities. The rapacity (sometimes called "state prize") effect refers to the idea that valuable economic resources can provide an incentive to fight over their control. And the resource effect recognizes that both government and rebels may fund their activities by taxing the production of commodities, so that changes in their value affect the ability to sustain conflict.

The empirical results provide strong support for the rapacity effect. Increases in the prices of exported oil and mineral commodities substantially raise the risk conflict. An increase in the value of these exports of 10 percent raises the risk of conflict by 2.2 percent on average across countries. This is due to the rapacity effect. The higher the value of resources that can be easily appropriated through fighting, such as minerals and oil, the greater is the incentive to fight over them. The finding from Nigerian states is similar: a 10 percent increase in the price of oil raises the number of conflict events by 2 percent. These results are also consistent with other intra-country evidence from Colombia (Dube and Vargas 2013), the Democratic Republic of Congo (Maystadt et al. 2014), and from Sub-Saharan Africa (Berman et al. 2014).

When the Nigerian government started using some of the oil revenues to demobilize and reintegrate the militants in the oil-producing regions, the positive relation between oil price and conflict intensity disappeared. That followed the agreement in 2009, whereby the federal state granted amnesty and provided employment to the militants in those states. This finding supports the "resource effect," which recognizes that the government (and sometimes also the rebels) may fund their activities by taxing the production of commodities, so that changes in their value affect the ability to repress or buy off the rebels, at least in the short term.

On the other hand, the cross-country evidence provides little support for the opportunity cost hypothesis. Changes in the prices of agricultural exports, in the prices of imported commodities, and in export demand are not significantly related to the probability of conflict. By contrast, the country case studies provide strong support for the opportunity cost effect. This difference with the cross-country evidence is likely due to two reasons. First, the availability of data within countries allows one to isolate the impact of commodity price changes on real incomes. Second, the large heterogeneity across countries can mask effects that may be important within individual countries. In Nigeria, conflict is significantly related to changes in real incomes driven by commodity indexes that reflect both production (higher prices, less conflict) and consumption (higher prices, more conflict) by the households. The importance of changes in real incomes in affecting conflict also applies to the Boko Haram attacks since 2010. The opportunity cost hypothesis holds in the West Bank and Gaza, where exogenous sectoral increases in export revenues were associated with subsequent lower levels of conflict during the Second Intifada in localities where private sector employment in that sector was significant. These findings confirm the evidence emerging from other within-country studies (e.g., Dube and Vargas 2013; Berman and Couttenier 2014).[4]

Intense trading with neighbors reduces the duration as well as the intensity of conflict. This trade reduces the incentives of contiguous countries to fuel civil conflict in their neighbors similarly to the case of inter-state wars. These incentives may be particularly strong in areas, such as much of sub-Saharan Africa, where there are strong ethnic ties across borders. Trading with neighbors is also associated with a lower risk of conflict when such trade occurs under regional trade agreements.

The strength of the effect of commodity exports on conflict varies across and within countries and depends on a number of local conditions. Changes in economic conditions have a much greater potential for generating conflict where there are deep-seated, historical grievances among groups, where economic inequality is high, and where government institutions are weak or corrupt. The report identifies four groups of local conditions that may affect the relationship between changes in trade flows and conflict: (i) grievances that foster tensions among groups, for example generated by economic inequality, ethnic and religious differences, or past conflict events; (ii) the state's institutional capacity and the form of political arrangements, for example democratic versus authoritarian rule; (iii) conditions in neighboring countries, for example the level of violence, that might encourage or discourage conflict in the country of interest; and (iv) policies that affect the transmission of changes in international commodity prices to the domestic market.

The cross-country analysis suggests that grievances—stemming from ethnic divisions, income inequality, and a past history of conflict—and the presence of a conflict in neighboring countries have a particularly significant impact on the relationship between changes in trade and conflict. While the quality of governance also helps reduce the effects of trade shocks on conflict, the impact of political arrangements is more limited. And interventions that slow the transmission of changes in international commodity prices to domestic markets appear to reduce the risk of conflict from changes in export prices, although not for point-source commodities.

Similar, although not identical, results emerge from the country case studies. In Nigeria, the impact of commodity price swings on conflict is greater in election years, in states with high levels of ethnic divisions and inequality, and it is smaller in states that are farther from Lagos (which tends to reduce the transmission of international commodity price changes to local markets). Interestingly, past incidents of violence are not shown to increase the impact of commodity prices on conflict. In the West Bank and Gaza, the impact of changes in exports on conflict is increased by the existence of grievances such as the presence of refugees, high unemployment rates, and a potential indicator of the number of inhabitants in Israeli jails, but not the incidence of violent fatalities in the past or the level of education.

Policy Directions

Following the analysis and the review of the evidence, the report highlights five general policy directions to use trade to support stability, arguably the most important direct policy objective in fragile countries. These include both trade-related and complementary policies.

Limit government (and rebels') access to and discretion over the spending of the revenues from point-source commodities. Examples of policy options in line with these principles include: a) improving transparency of the size and use of these revenues, for example by centralizing government collection of the revenues and by cooperating with international transparency initiatives; b) paying a portion of the revenues directly to citizens or transferring the revenues to producing areas (the former could enhance the oversight of the use of revenues and create incentives to resist efforts to increase government or rebel control over resources; the latter could reduce resentment in producing areas and compensate for the economic disruption and environmental degradation that often accompanies the exploitation of oil or minerals); c) channeling the resource revenues through external financial vehicles, such as sovereign wealth funds (although the record of such vehicles is mixed).

Protect the real incomes of producers, consumers, and workers from adverse changes in trade flows. Targeted transfers, public works programs, price subsidies, and temporary trade insulation are potential options to achieve this objective. All of these policies have strengths and weaknesses, but some evidence suggests that targeted transfers—albeit challenging to develop—appear to be particularly useful in counteracting the losses by households as a result of an adverse trade change (Anderson, Ivanic, and Martin 2013; Attanasio et al. 2013).

Promote labor-intensive exports. This requires two main, mutually reinforcing strategies. The first is to increase fragile countries' market access in goods and services in labor intensive sectors in the main trading partners. The second is to enhance the relative competitiveness of fragile countries' exports, particularly in labor intensive sectors. This requires a broad set of interventions to improve trade connectivity and firms' productivity (Reis and Farole 2012). In conflict affected and post-conflict environments, both areas are usually deficient due to the destruction and insecurity caused by the conflict.

Strengthen trading relations with neighbors. Both trade policy and trade facilitation can help foster trade relations among neighbors. There is abundant evidence of the existence of high policy barriers to trade, especially between fragile countries. Such barriers even constrain trade in basic food staples between sub-Saharan African neighbors (World Bank 2012). While necessary, efficient trade policy is not sufficient to stimulate trade between neighboring fragile countries, most of which—as this report shows—are marred by particularly poor transit, logistics, and transport infrastructure systems.

Focus on the broader agenda of reducing some of the structural determinants of conflict at the country level. That agenda is consistent with some of the principles highlighted by the World Bank (2011a), and encompasses: tackling ethnic divisions, reducing economic inequalities, resolving tensions from past conflicts, strengthening accountability, and the control of corruption. Building these conditions requires a longer term horizon than is usually adopted by a government legislature. Yet investing in them is also likely to be necessary in order to permanently break the conflict trap.

The international community, including the World Bank Group, can help fragile countries use trade to fight fragility by focusing on certain areas. Key areas for international support include the provision of technical assistance to improve trade facilitation and export competitiveness in fragile countries, and to enhance transparency concerning the size and use of resource revenues; assistance with arrangements to limit government discretion over resource revenues; the financing of programs to protect real incomes from adverse changes in trade flows; and the provision of improved market access in both goods and services for fragile countries.

This report is composed of three main chapters. Chapter 1 develops a conceptual framework mapping the different channels through which trade may affect conflict and political stability. The framework is based on simple economic theory and the available empirical evidence on the impact of trade-related changes on conflict and stability. It then tests this framework empirically through the analysis of cross-country data and through case studies of Nigeria and the Israeli-Palestinian conflict. The hope is that these types of intra-country analyses could be replicated in other countries, since they use data that are available in different countries, especially in sub-Saharan Africa. Chapter 2 uses the same conceptual framework to show how differences in underlying conditions affect the relationship between trade-related changes and conflict. Following a review of the literature on the drivers of conflict, it examines the importance of four groups of grievances: conditions in neighboring countries, factors increasing grievance, government institutions, and policies that affect the transmission of changes in international prices to the domestic market. These relationships are tested using cross-country data and case studies of Nigeria and the Israeli-Palestinian conflict. Finally, chapter 3 uses the existing evidence, as well as evidence generated in this report, to discuss how the policies governing trade can reduce the probability and intensity of conflicts. Two appendixes include detailed information on the modeling framework, the data issues and the estimation results.

Notes

1. Fragile countries in this case are defined according to the OECD list (see box 1.1 in chapter 1).

2. The list of these fragile countries is slightly different from that maintained by the OECD and comes from the World Bank African Development Bank and Asian Development Bank Harmonized List of Fragile Situations, discussed in box 1.1.

3. According to the Failed States Index 2013 (Fund for Peace 2013), three quarters of the twenty countries most at risk of conflict are in sub-Saharan Africa.

4. The cross-country study provides little support for the opportunity cost hypothesis. The difference with the within country evidence is likely to be due to two reasons. First the availability of data within countries enables us to isolate the impact of commodity price changes on real incomes. Second, the large heterogeneity across countries can mask effects that may be important within individual countries.

References

Anderson, K., M. Ivanic, and W. Martin. 2013. "Food Price Spikes, Price Insulation and Poverty." World Bank, Mimeo.

Attanasio, O., V. Di Maro, V. Lechene, and D. Phillips. 2013. "Welfare Consequences of Food Prices Increases: Evidence from Rural Mexico." *Journal of Development Economics* 104: 136–51.

Berman, N., and M. Couttenier. 2014. "External Shocks, Internal Shots: The Geography of Civil Conflicts." CEPR Discussion Paper 9895.

Berman, N., M. Couttenier, D. Rohner, and M. Thoenig. 2014. "This Mine Is Mine! How Minerals Fuel Conflicts in Africa." OxCarre Research Paper 141.

Dube, O., and J. Vargas. 2013. "Commodity Price Shocks and Civil Conflict: Evidence from Colombia." *Review of Economic Studies* 80 (4): 1384–421.

Fund for Peace. 2013. "The Failed States Index 2013." http://ffp.statesindex.org /rankings-2013-sortable.

Lakner, C., M. Negre, and E. B. Prydz. 2014. "Twinning the Goals: How Can Shared Prosperity Help Reduce Global Poverty?" Policy Research Working Paper, World Bank, forthcoming.

Maystadt, J-F., G. De Luca, P. G. Sekeris, J. Ulimwengu, and R. Folledo. 2014. "Mineral Resources and Conflicts in DRC: A Case of Ecological Fallacy?" *Oxford Economic Papers* 66 (3): 721–49. http://oep.oxfordjournals.org/content/66/3/721.

Reis, J. G., and T. Farole. 2012. *Trade Competitiveness Diagnostic Toolkit*. Washington, DC: World Bank.

World Bank. 2011a. *World Development Report 2011: Conflict, Security and Development*. Washington, DC: World Bank.

———. 2011b. *Middle East and North Africa: Facing Challenges and Opportunities*. Economic Developments and Prospects Report.

———. 2012. *Africa Can Help Feed Africa*. Washington, DC: World Bank.

CHAPTER 1

How Trade Can Affect Conflict

Introduction

On the face of it, it may be difficult to believe that the horrific experiences of civil war that have plagued many poor countries over the past decades are influenced by changes in international commodity prices or external demand for a country's exports. Nevertheless, there are many recent examples of civil conflicts where economic motivations, along with others, appear to have played an important role. A growing economic literature has elaborated theories of how changes in external trade may drive conflict onset, intensity, or duration, and has tested these theories. On the basis of this literature, this chapter aims to provide an analytical framework for thinking about how changes in trade flows may affect conflict, and to test this model against experiences across countries, and across regions in two case studies (Nigeria and the West Bank and Gaza).

One reason that trade flows can have such an important impact on conflict in fragile countries is that they are much larger than other external flows and can have very large effects on real incomes. While trade can make an enormous contribution to development by encouraging the reallocation of resources to more productive activities, changes in relative prices as a result of trade may also involve losses by workers (and their families) in declining sectors. Such losses may be short-lived, as workers in declining sectors take up other activities that may have benefited from the change in trade flows. However, the poor economic environment (weak rule of law, low levels of education and training, underdeveloped financial sectors) in fragile countries often limits workers' ability to take advantage of the opportunities opened by trade. Thus the losses in real incomes as a result of trade can be significant and long-lasting in fragile countries. Trade in fragile countries can also be more volatile than other sources of foreign exchange, in part because exports are highly concentrated in primary commodities, many of which are subject to large and frequent fluctuations in price. Moreover, fragile countries are highly dependent on food imports, where changes in prices can have immediate—and at times dire—implications for large portions of the population.

Abrupt changes in trade can affect conflict through three distinct mechanisms. The opportunity cost mechanism refers to the tendency for declines in real incomes to reduce the income foregone by those choosing to engage in conflict. Thus declines in export prices, increases in import prices, and declines in external demand that reduce real incomes are associated with greater conflict. The rapacity effect describes how increases in price can encourage violent competition for point-source commodities, for example oil or diamonds. And the resource effect refers to how increases in the value of goods subject to government (or rebel) taxation can provide the means to suppress (or enhance) violence.

While these three motivations are analytically distinct, measuring them is particularly challenging. First, changes in the value of some commodities can have cross-cutting effects. For example, a rise in the price of an export commodity that is also consumed may raise producers' real incomes but reduce the real incomes of consuming households. Thus, even if the opportunity cost mechanism is important in motivating participation (or not) in conflict, it may be difficult to identify this in the data. Second, the impact on conflict of trade changes may differ depending on differences in local conditions. An increase in oil exports may boost conflict in oil-producing Nigeria, but not in oil-producing Norway.

The cross-country analysis in this chapter finds the strongest evidence for the rapacity effect. In a significant departure from some of the most recent literature, we find that price swings of exported commodities do matter for the probability of conflict. An exogenous increase in the value of a country's exported commodities raises the probability of a civil conflict erupting in that country. The effect is far from negligible: an increase of 10 percent in the value of exports raises the risk of conflict by between 2.2 and 2.5 percentage points. This result is primarily driven by competition for point-source commodities that experience rising prices.

By contrast, the cross-country evidence provides little support for the view that conflict is fueled by reductions in real income due to commodity price changes (the opportunity cost mechanism). Neither changes in the prices of export commodities that are not the potential objects of predation, nor the prices of imported commodities, nor changes in demand in export markets appear to exert any influence on the probability or the duration of conflict. However, the cross-country estimations do provide some indication that export and import prices may affect conflict intensity in the direction anticipated by the opportunity cost theory. This confirms previous evidence that triggering a new conflict is more difficult than escalating an existing one (Bazzi and Blattman 2014).

The country case studies provide clearer evidence of the opportunity cost effect, in part because of the availability of more detailed data than is feasible in cross-country analysis (Blattman and Miguel 2010). In Nigeria, data on the commodity composition of household consumption and production allows the construction of price indices that accurately reflect the impact of commodity price changes on real incomes. The estimations find that increases in the prices of commodities that are important in household production (consumption) are negatively (positively) associated with conflict. Measuring how changes in commodity prices affect both production and consumption (which many studies fail to do) is critical to accurately identifying the importance of the opportunity cost effect in driving conflict.

The Nigeria analysis also finds evidence of the rapacity effect through the positive impact of rising oil prices on conflict. However, this effect disappears when considering the period after the amnesty deal was signed between the state and the militant groups in the Niger Delta, suggesting that the state may have been able to use oil revenues to counteract the rapacity effect, at least in the short run. Changes in the prices of both production and consumption items also have had a major impact on the intensity of the Boko Haram conflict since 2010.

In the West Bank and Gaza, sharp changes in export revenues in the late 1990s were driven by the emergence of new foreign suppliers, chiefly China, and the Israeli trade liberalization, which reduced Palestinians' preferential access to the Israeli market. Information on these changes in export revenues by economic sector are linked to data on the sectoral composition of employment in each locality. An increase of $10 million in export revenues (before the Second Intifada) in a sector that accounts for at least 10 percent of private employment in a locality reduces the number of conflict-related fatalities in that locality (during the Second Intifada) by 2.1 percent. The finding that improved employment prospects are linked to lower conflict-related fatalities supports the opportunity cost hypothesis. The fact that Palestinian exports do not include point-source commodities facilitated identifying the importance of the opportunity cost effect.

Trading with neighboring countries was also found to be significantly related to conflict. Higher levels of trade with neighbors reduce the duration, as well as the intensity, of conflict, because such trade reduces the incentives of contiguous countries to fuel conflict in their neighbors. Importantly, trading with neighbors is also associated with a lower risk of conflict when such trade occurs under regional trade agreements (RTAs), although it is hard to determine causality for this result. Further, the incidence of conflict in neighboring countries is significantly and positively related to conflict in the country of interest. The influence of neighboring countries on conflict is a frequently observed characteristic of many modern conflicts.

Of course, civil war does not occur in a vacuum, and changes in trade prices and volumes that may spur conflict in some contexts may have no impact at all on conflict in others. Diamonds have been a curse in Angola but a blessing in Botswana. Chapter 2 is devoted to understanding how different factors may affect the relationship between changes in trade flows and conflict.

The next section of the chapter argues that the size, volatility, and limited diversification of trade flows in fragile countries may magnify their impact on civil conflict. The section titled "Why Changes in Trade Flows May Affect Conflict" outlines an analytical framework that details the channels through which changes in trade flows affect decisions on whether to engage in civil violence. The section on "Cross-Country Evidence on Trade Shocks and Conflict" tests this framework, using a dataset on the occurrence of civil conflict across countries. The section on "Evidence from Nigerian States" applies a similar empirical test to the incidence of conflict across regions in Nigeria, and the section on "Evidence from the Israeli-Palestinian Conflict" does the same for the West Bank and Gaza.

Trade Flows in Fragile Countries Are Different

Sharp changes in trade prices and volumes can be an important trigger of instability in fragile countries (see box 1.1 for a definition of fragile countries). Trade flows in these countries are much larger than other sources of foreign exchange (i.e. official development assistance—ODA, remittances, and foreign direct investment—FDI) (figure 1.1). Trade in fragile countries is also more volatile than these other foreign exchange flows. FDI, ODA, and remittances to fragile countries exhibited little volatility and increased steadily from 2000 to 2010. Remittances, for example, rose from just under $9 billion in 2000 to over $47 billion by 2010 (OECD 2013). By contrast, trade flows have fluctuated to a larger degree, and these swings have resulted in much larger absolute changes than for any other external flow. For example, the global crisis reduced the trade-GDP ratio in fragile countries with available data by almost 10 percentage points in 2009, and the dollar value of the fall in trade was almost half the total value of other inflows to fragile countries.

Box 1.1 Which Are the Fragile Countries?

There is no consensus in the development community on what specific characteristics are necessary to classify a country as fragile, which has led to varying definitions and lists of fragile countries. However, each definition is predicated to some degree on the existence, relative weakness, or lack of governance and institutional capacity.

For example, the joint World Bank/African Development Bank/Asian Development Bank Harmonized List of Fragile and Conflict-Affected Situations (FCS) includes all low-income countries and territories eligible for World Bank assistance with a score of 3.2 or lower on the internally generated Country Policy and Institutional Assessment (CPIA),[a] a diagnostic tool intended to measure the policies, institutional arrangements, and other key elements within a country's control that support sustainable growth, poverty reduction, and the effective use of development assistance.[b] It also includes countries with the presence of a regional or UN peacekeeping mission within the last three years.

The OECD extends this list to cover states meeting the following definition of fragility: "a state is understood to be fragile when it is unable to meet its population's expectations or manage changes in expectation and capacity through the political process."[c] The OECD's most recent list of 51 fragile countries is a compilation of two lists: the aforementioned Harmonized List of Fragile Situations, as well as the 2011 Failed States Index (FSI), prepared by the Fund for Peace and published by *Foreign Policy*. The OECD estimates that although "one-fifth (about 18.5 percent) of the world's population lived in fragile states in 2010, these countries hosted about one-third of the world's poor (400 million out of 1.2 billion)" (OECD 2013).

Other, reasonable criteria for defining fragility could encompass even more countries. It is well documented, for instance, that countries which have recently experienced conflict are more likely to relapse into conflict (World Bank 2011). One approach to capturing this higher risk in a definition of fragility is to take into account the number of recent battlefield deaths. Between 2005 and 2010, Sri Lanka and Pakistan—neither of which appears on the World Bank's

box continues next page

Box 1.1 Which Are the Fragile Countries? *(continued)*

list of fragile countries—experienced 8,413 and 6,688 battlefield deaths in a single year, respectively. Both figures exceed the single-year total of 6,238 recorded in Afghanistan, which topped the World Bank's list of "deadliest" fragile states during that period. Table A.1 in appendix A lists the countries considered fragile by the World Bank (in 2013), alongside a list of other countries with at least one year of minor conflict (measured according to the Gleditsch et al. (2002) definition as a year with at least 25 battlefield deaths) from 2005 to 2010.

a. See http://go.worldbank.org/NEK8GNPSO0.
b. http://go.worldbank.org/EEAIU81ZG0.
c. OECD glossary of International Network on Conflict and Fragility (INCAF) terms, http://www.oecd.org/document/13/0,3746,
en_2649_33693550_49377421_1_1_1_1,00.html.

Figure 1.1 Trade Represents the Major Source of Foreign Exchange in Fragile States
Percent of GDP

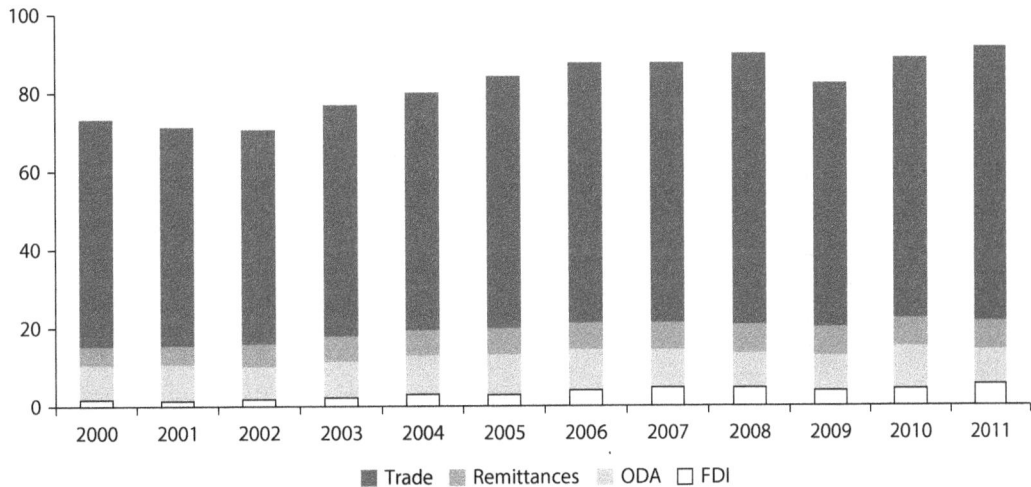

Sources: World Development Indicators; Reflects 22 countries from the 2015 OECD list of fragile states for which data were available.
Note: Trade is defined as exports of goods and services plus imports of goods and services. FDI = foreign direct investment; ODA = official development assistance.

Fragile countries may be more vulnerable to changes in trade flows than many other developing countries, due to low levels of export diversification. Fragile countries' export markets and products are more concentrated than in other developing countries (table 1.1).[1] In more than half of the fragile countries with adequate data, the largest export accounts for over a quarter of merchandise exports (figure 1.2). Several fragile countries' exports are dominated by only a few products to a much greater extent than comparable nonfragile countries (figure 1.3). For example, in 2010, T-shirts, sweatshirts, and suits accounted for 76 percent of Haiti's exports; 87 percent of exports from the

**Table 1.1 Fragile Countries' Exports Are Less Diversified Than Other Developing Countries'
Exports**

Index of concentration

Type of diversification	Year	Mean	Median
Market (fragile states)	2012	0.26	0.21
Market (all developing countries)	2012	0.24	0.17
Product (fragile states)	2012	0.33	0.21
Product (all developing countries)	2012	0.25	0.16

Source: Authors' elaboration based on UN Commodity Trade Statistics Database (HS 6 digit product classification).
Note: fragile states based on the OECD's list of fragile states. The index is a flow-weighted concentration index normalized to range between 0 and 1, with a higher level indicating higher concentration. Due to lack of some country's export data, "mirror data" is used (partner's imports from that country).

Figure 1.2 Share of Largest Exports in Selected Fragile Countries and Territories (in 2010)

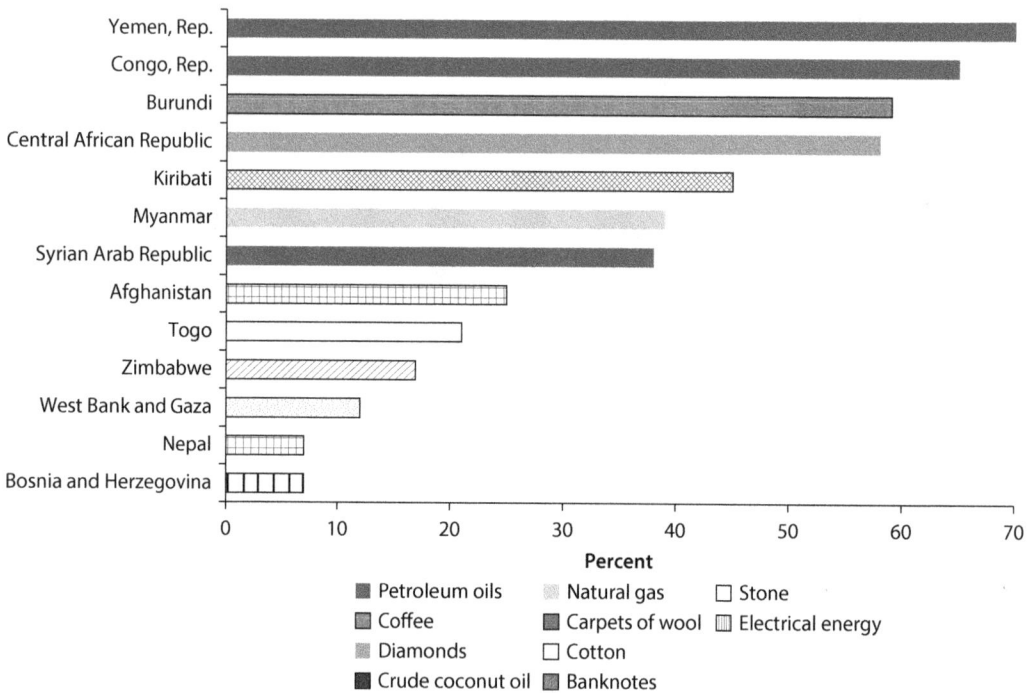

Legend:
■ Petroleum oils   Natural gas   □ Stone
■ Coffee   ■ Carpets of wool   ▦ Electrical energy
Diamonds   □ Cotton
■ Crude coconut oil   ▦ Banknotes

Source: Authors' elaboration based on UN Commodity Trade Statistics Database.

Central African Republic were wrapped up in only four product lines: diamonds (32 percent), raw wood (30 percent), sawn/chipped wood (15 percent), and cotton (10 percent); and Iraq's economy relies for all intents and purposes solely on crude oil.[2] On the other hand other developing countries (Honduras, Moldova, and Peru) with similar population to each of these countries (but with higher GDP per capita) have a considerably more diversified export basket (figure 1.3).

Figure 1.3 For Many Fragile States, Exports Are Not Heavily Diversified

a. Haiti
Total: $968M

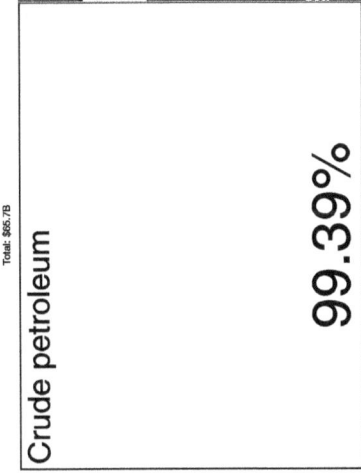

b. Central African Republic
Total: $207M

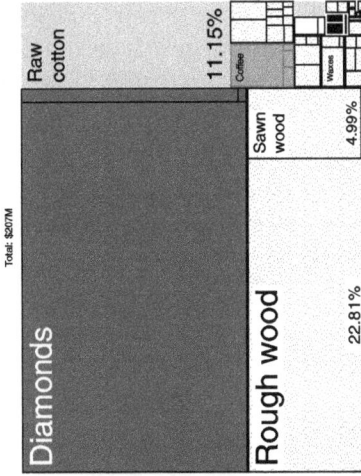

c. Iraq
Total: $65.7B

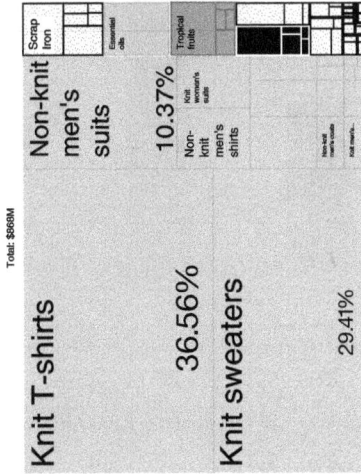

d. Honduras
Total: $8.33B

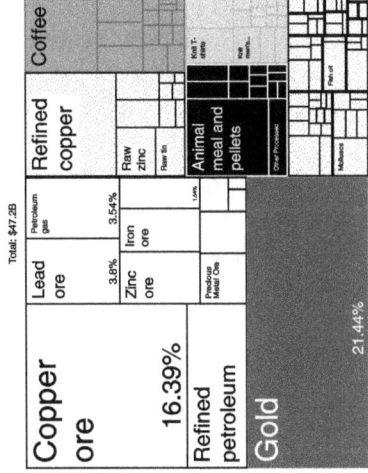

e. Moldova
Total: $2.77B

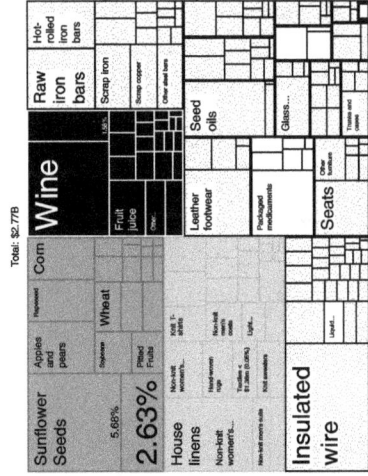

f. Peru
Total: $47.2B

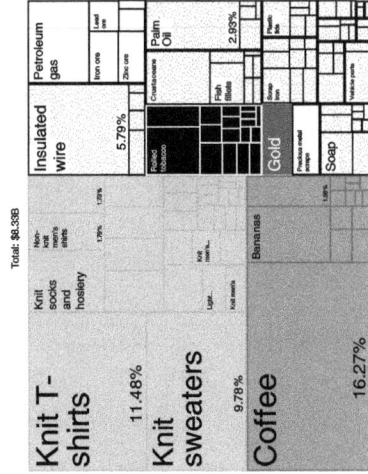

Source: MIT's Observatory of Economic Complexity at atlas.media.mit.edu.

Moreover, fragile countries are highly dependent on primary commodity exports, which are subject to considerable price volatility. Sharp changes in international commodity prices can have important implications for employment, income, and investment in fragile countries. For example, exports from Benin, Chad, and Mali grew by 30 percent following the increase in the world price of cotton from 1994 to 1996 and declined by as much as 20 percent with the drop in cotton prices between 1997 and 1999 (FAO 2002).

In addition, fragile countries' high levels of food imports contribute to food insecurity (Aksoy and Ng 2008). Food accounted for nearly 17 percent of all fragile country imports in 2010, compared to less than 14 percent for other developing countries.[3] To the extent that international food price variability can be a destabilizing factor (Arezki and Brückner 2011), this higher dependence on food imports can increase the sensitivity of fragile countries to trade shocks (figure 1.4).

Compounding these problems, fragile countries also perform particularly poorly in terms of trade facilitation. A fragile country has lower scores on every available indicator of trade facilitation relative to a country in the same region and income group (left panel in figure 1.5). This penalty varies between 5 percent and 8 percent for the Logistics Performance Indicator (LPI) and between 7 percent and 12 percent for the perception index of port

Figure 1.4 For Fragile States, Net Food Imports Constitute a Higher Percentage of GDP

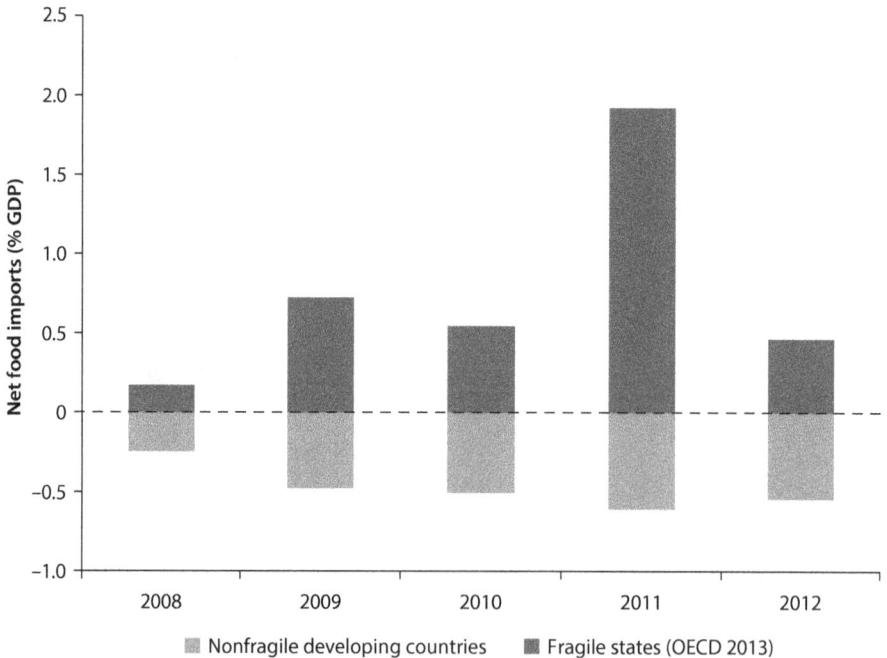

Sources: Author calculations based on UN COMTRADE data (via WITS) and WDI data.

Figure 1.5 Fragile Countries Perform Worse Than Their Peers in Trade Facilitation and the Gap Is Growing

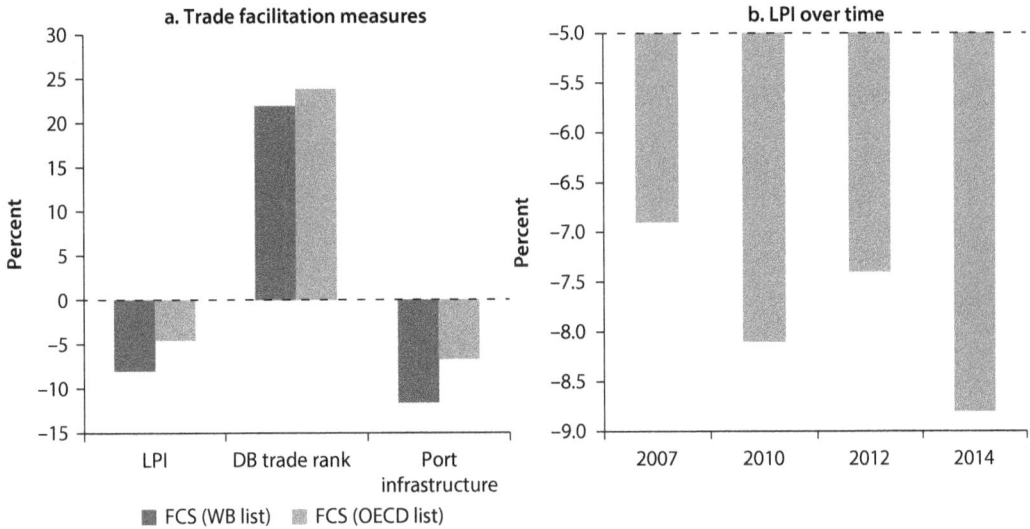

Note: In the left panel the y-axis measures the average percentage difference of fragile countries relative to their income and regional peers across various indicators of trade facilitation (World Bank 2014c), rank of World Bank Doing Business Trading Across Borders indicators (World Bank 2014a), and World Economic Forum perception of port infrastructure quality (World Economic Forum 2014). This penalty is computed as the coefficient of a fragile country dummy in a regression of the log of the indicator on income group, regional and year dummies as well as the fragile dummy. Only countries for which LPI data are available in all years are included (constant sample of 130 countries). In the right panel the y-axis measures the average percentage penalty of fragile countries (according to the World Bank list) relative to their income and regional peers (only countries for which LPI data are available in all years are included, yielding a constant sample of 130 countries). All data on indicators come from World Bank (2014b) except for the 2014 LPI data, which come from World Bank (2014c).

infrastructure according to the fragile classification one uses (i.e. OECD or World Bank/regional development banks list). Similarly, being a fragile country is associated with a 22–24 percent higher rank in the Doing Business "Trading Across Borders" ranking (again relative to a similar countries for per capita income and regional group). Worryingly, this penalty has been increasing over time in terms of the LPI, which is the indicator with the greatest coverage of countries-years (right panel in figure 1.5). This poor trade facilitation performance makes export growth and diversification even more challenging for fragile countries. In addition it creates a further penalty for the consumers in these countries relying on imported goods.

The combination of heavy reliance on exports as a source of foreign exchange, limited export diversification, reliance on volatile primary commodity exports, and dependence on food imports means that trade can play a major role in triggering conflict in fragile countries. However, even large, abrupt changes in trade flows, by themselves, do not cause conflicts. Rather, changes in trade can interact with existing tensions, for example ethnic rivalries or regional differences, which may well be sufficient to incite conflict on their own. The next sections will try to disentangle the channels through which changes in trade can affect country stability. Chapter 2 considers the conditions which make countries more sensitive to these shocks.

Why Changes in Trade Flows May Affect Conflict

There are at least three main mechanisms through which economic shocks, including trade-related changes, can affect political instability. We refer to these as opportunity cost, rapacity, and resource effects.

First, changes in trade flows can change real incomes. As in Becker's (1968) seminal work on the economics of crime, an individual's real income can be seen as his opportunity cost of engaging in a rebellious activity.[4] For example, a fall in the price of a key export commodity can reduce employment in that sector, thus reducing the income that workers in that sector must forfeit by engaging in conflict. Alternatively, rising prices of a commodity important for household production will increase the household's income and reduce their willingness to participate in conflict. More generally, the opportunity cost mechanism describes how changes in real incomes affect the willingness to participate in conflict through changing the relative return on conflict activities compared to more peaceful pursuits. This relatively dry language should not be taken to imply that the choice to participate in conflict is free of compulsion. A father who joins a rebel group after his livelihood is destroyed and his family begins to starve is motivated by what we call the opportunity cost mechanism. But he may perceive little choice in the matter. We should also note that a decline in real incomes may also encourage violence due to the resentment and frustration from experiencing a fall in social status or a deteriorating ability to care for one's family, driven by economic forces over which the individual lacks any control.

Second, civil conflicts are also fought over the control of valuable economic resources. The rapacity effect refers to the willingness to engage in conflict to control the production of commodities, such as oil or minerals, which do not require massive amounts of labor, are highly valuable, are not perishable, and are easily controlled. These point-source resources are generally traded in international markets and subject to large swings in prices that affect their value, and thus the willingness to fight to obtain them. In addition to purely economic motives, individuals may turn to violence to protest the often serious social and environmental consequences of the exploitation of oil or minerals. However, the evidence presented in the remainder of the report is more consistent with the rapacity effect than with these environmental and social consequences.

Third, the resource effect refers to how changes in the value of traded goods will affect civil conflicts if the state or the rebels can rely on them to fund violent activities. For example, the government may be able to capture substantial revenues from oil rents, or rebels may be able to extract a portion of increased agricultural prices from farmers in areas they control.

It is useful to distinguish between three types of trade-related change that affect conflict: 1) changes in international commodity prices; 2) changes in trading conditions; and 3) changes in trade with neighboring countries. Figure 1.6 links these changes to the incentives of the actors to engage in conflict through the three mechanisms described above. We explore the effects of each type of change in turn.

Figure 1.6 Mapping the Linkages between Changes in Trade Flows and Civil Conflict

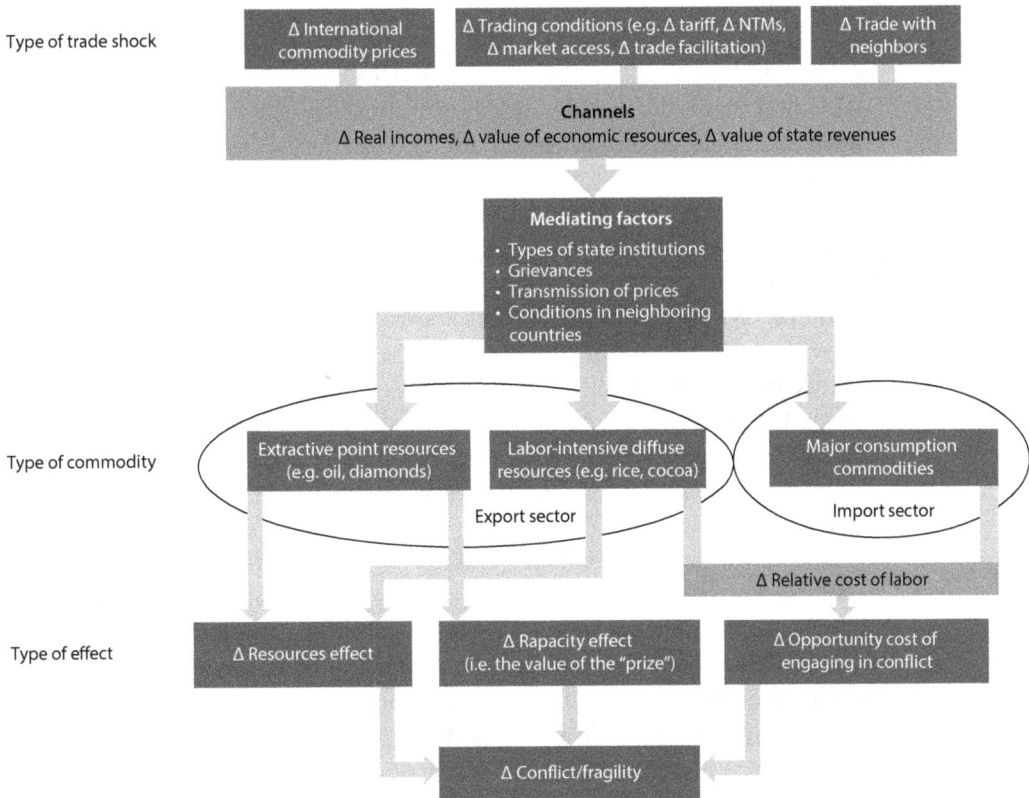

Commodity Export Prices

Changes in international commodity prices have drawn the most attention in the literature examining the impact of trade-related changes on conflict. Although the focus of the literature has been mainly on the export side, these price changes are likely to have an impact via the import side as well.

Changes in the international price of an export commodity may affect incentives to engage in conflict through the three mechanisms given above (opportunity cost, rapacity, and resources). As in the case of other changes in real incomes, the potential for changes in commodity prices to affect conflict has received mixed empirical support. Bruckner and Ciccone (2010) find that a reduction in the international price of a country's main commodity export leads to a higher chance of civil conflict in sub-Saharan Africa. Savun and Tirone (2012) show similar evidence for a larger sample of countries. This relationship is generally supported in recent within-country work, which studies the variation in conflict and production across subnational units. Dube and Vargas (2013), for example, find that during the 1990s a reduction in the price of coffee, the largest labor-intensive commodity exported by Colombia, increased the intensity of conflict by more in the municipalities specialized in coffee production than in the others. Using data on small subunits across 48 sub-Saharan African countries, Berman and Couttenier (2014) find that an increase in a region's main agricultural commodity exports (measured by data on imports from partner countries) decreases the probability of a conflict and its intensity. Maystadt and Ecker (2014) find that reductions in the price of livestock (driven by droughts rather than international markets) substantially increase the incidence of conflict across regions in Somalia.

On the other hand, evidence from other cross-country studies does not support the view that declines in real income are associated with greater willingness to participate in civil conflicts (the opportunity cost mechanism). Besley and Persson (2008) find that the price of exported commodities is positively associated with the incidence of civil conflict, a result that the authors interpret as evidence of the rapacity effect. Bazzi and Blattman (2014) find no robust relationship between changes in the international prices of commodity exports and either the beginning or ending of conflict across a large sample of developing countries, although they do find some evidence that these price changes may affect conflict intensity.

These contrasting cross-country findings suggest that the impact of commodity prices on conflict varies substantially by the type of commodity (and according to local conditions, an issue we address in chapter 2). Indeed, the conceptual framework illustrated above suggests that all commodities are not created equal when it comes to their effects on conflict: increases in the value of some commodities may increase conflict through the rapacity effect, while increases in the value of others may reduce (or increase) conflict through the opportunity cost mechanism. A rise in the price of a commodity whose control can be relatively easily appropriated can foster conflict by increasing the potential prize of the conflict, thus raising the incentive for fighting (the rapacity effect). This is usually the case for so-called point-source resources such as minerals and fuels, which are contestable, highly valuable, capital-intensive, and geographically concentrated resources. At the other end of the spectrum, increases in the price of what we refer to as "diffuse" commodities (often agricultural commodities) that are important in household production and are produced over wide areas, labor intensive, and more difficult (though not impossible) to control, may reduce conflict by raising the opportunity cost of participating in a rebellion. Dal Bó and Dal Bó (2011) develop a general equilibrium model to formalize this intuition.

The "rapacity effect" is part of the explanation for the eruption and/or the escalation of violence in many modern conflicts. As in the case of the opportunity cost mechanism, the evidence in support of the rapacity effect is stronger within countries than across them. Maystadt et al. (2014) show that new mining concessions spurred by increases in international mineral prices increase the level of violence across districts in the Democratic Republic of Congo. Similarly, Dube and Vargas (2013) find that increases in oil prices are associated with higher violence across Colombian municipalities. Bellows and Miguel (2009) show that the presence of diamonds was associated with higher violence during the civil war in Sierra Leone.[5]

Other cross-country studies provide some evidence on the conflict-inducing effects of oil resources in Africa (Buhaug and Rod 2006) and in low-income countries (Lin and Michaels 2011).[6] On the other hand, neither Cotet and Tsui (2013) nor Bazzi and Blattman (2014) find any cross-country evidence supportive of the hypothesis that larger values of extractive resources are associated with higher levels of conflict. One reason for these mixed results could be that increases in value of disputable resources can generate higher fiscal revenues. The state could use these revenues to strengthen its military capacity to repress rebel groups' activities and/or to buy off support, thus favoring political stability.[7]

On the other hand, prices of diffused agricultural commodities may be negatively related to conflict. Their production is labor intensive and more difficult than point-source commodities for the government to tax. Thus rising prices of diffuse commodities should raise incomes, thus increasing the opportunity cost of conflict. However, revenues from diffused commodities (as well as from mining activities) can also be an important source of funding for rebel groups controlling local areas. For example, in Myanmar the production and trade of timber and other agricultural products, as well as of mining products in the bordering areas with Thailand and China, was taxed by local rebel groups fighting the central government.[8] Whether on balance rising prices of diffuse agricultural commodities reduce conflict by increasing the opportunity cost facing would-be rebels, or increase conflict by helping to fund rebel groups, is an empirical question. In the case of the Colombian conflict the opportunity cost channel appears to be dominant for legal crops such as coffee and bananas (Dube and Vargas 2013), while the rebel funding mechanism is more important for coca production (Angrist and Kugler 2008).

Another potentially important distinction is between commodities that are important consumption items domestically (e.g. rice and fuel) and those that are not (e.g. diamonds and cocoa). A rise in price would benefit producers, but would also penalize consumers, potentially sparking unrest. It is possible that the majority of households are net consumers in countries that are net exporters of that commodity. It is important to take into account this distributional impact of price changes in the identification of the effects on conflict. Bellemare (2011) provides some support for this relationship by linking monthly spikes in international food prices with increased political unrest worldwide.

This classification, as well as the distinction between point-source and diffuse commodities, generates a matrix of four types of export commodities (table 1.2). The empirical analysis below tests for differences in the effects of price changes on conflict across these groups of commodities.

Table 1.2 Classification of the Export Commodities (with Example)

	Point-source	Diffuse
Consumed	Oil	Rice
Not consumed	Diamonds	Cocoa

Prices of Imported Consumption Goods

The economic literature on the impact of commodity price changes on conflict has focused mostly on the prices of fragile countries' exports. Nevertheless, changes in the international prices of imported commodities could affect consumers, and thus their incentive to participate in violence, as much as prices of exported commodities affect producers. The mechanisms at play are similar to those for commodity exports, but with opposite "signs." As the prices of commodities tend to be correlated, failure to consider imported commodities' prices may lead to a bias in the measurement of the effect on conflict of the prices of exported commodities. In line with these findings, our analysis considers also the impact of the price of imported commodities on conflict.

The size of these effects depends on the share in household consumption and production of the commodities whose international price has changed. Ivanic and Martin (2008) find, for a sample of low-income countries, that the hike in international staple food prices in 2007–08 induced much more frequent and larger poverty increases than poverty reductions in a sample of low-income countries. As discussed above, fragile countries are particularly vulnerable to such food price fluctuations, as most of them are net food importing countries. Aksoy and Ng (2008) argue that the international community's efforts in promoting food security should focus on conflict countries, which exhibit the largest food deficits in the broad category of net food importers.

Recent studies have found some empirical support for the idea that changes in international food prices have affected conflict in fragile countries. To the best of our knowledge there is no evidence on other imported commodities. Arezki and Bruckner (2011) find that increases in the prices of imported food led to higher levels of antigovernment riots and civil conflict in low-income countries from 1970 to 2007. By contrast, changes in imported food prices had no impact on conflict in high-income countries. Maystadt, Trinh Tan, and Breisinger (2014) show this effect to be particularly strong for Arab countries, which are major food importers. Bellemare (2011) uses a different strategy and shows that monthly spikes in international food prices between January 1990 and January 2011 led to increased political unrest worldwide (as measured by food-related riots).

Changes in Trading Conditions

The literature on the impact of changes in trade flows on conflict has focused mainly on swings in commodity prices. However, other trade-related changes, such as sharp changes in demand in destination markets, changes in a country's own trade policy and that of trading partners, and changes in the geography of trade also are potentially relevant for conflict.

Changes in trading conditions with main partners may affect conflict in ways analogous to changes in commodity prices. Consider, for example, a change in a country's access to a foreign market. A reduction in the preferential access to a major exporting market X for a country could reduce the country's exports to X, thereby also reducing the incomes and employment of those involved in the production of the goods exported to X.[9] In general, any trade-related change that has a large enough impact on domestic incomes and employment opportunities could generate the same effects on conflict as the commodity price changes described above.

We can identify four types of trade-related changes that may matter here:

1. changes in demand in a country's trading partners, which change the demand for products from that country;
2. changes in the country's access to international markets;
3. changes in the country's domestic level of protection of goods and services;
4. changes in trade facilitation.

Changes in (1) and (2) have analytically similar effects. Increases in the main trading partners' demand (e.g. as a consequence of a rise in income) would increase the demand for the country's goods and services, all else equal. Similarly, an improvement in the country's preferential access to its main markets (e.g. as a consequence of a bilateral trade agreement) would also raise the demand for the country's products. In terms of the conceptual framework described above, these increases in demand would have the same effects as a change in commodity prices. Therefore, it matters which type of export experiences the rise in demand. If the higher demand is for diffuse agricultural commodities, e.g. cocoa, or labor-intensive manufacturing, e.g. textiles, the rise in real incomes could increase the opportunity cost of conflict, thus reducing incentives to engage in conflict. If the higher demand is for point-source capital-intensive commodities, such as oil, then rising demand could increase conflict through the rapacity effect, by raising the value of the prize.

The limited evidence available supports the view that higher external demand for a country's exports reduces conflict. Bruckner and Ciccone (2010) find that economic downturns in the main OECD export destinations of sub-Saharan African countries' exports are associated with a higher probability of an outbreak of conflict. Chaudion, Peskowitz, and Stanton (2012) find similar effects on the onset as well as the intensity of conflict across a large sample of countries. Berman and Couttenier (2014) find evidence that banking crises that reduce demand in export destinations increase conflict. In the only study we have found that focuses on market access, Berman and Couttenier (2014) show that enhanced preferential access to the U.S. market through the Africa Growth and Opportunity Act (AGOA) reduced conflict across eight African countries, especially in those countries with a high share of exports in products eligible under AGOA. The finding that increases in demand are associated with a reduction in conflict is consistent with the fact that most of the agricultural and manufactured goods exported by fragile countries are relatively labor intensive, so that increases in their price directly benefit workers.

Another trade-related change to consider is the impact of a country's own trade policies on the production and consumption of traded goods. Trade restrictive measures, such as tariff increases or non-tariff measures (NTMs), may benefit those domestic producers who compete with imports. However, that advantage comes at the expense of higher prices facing the users of those products. Conversely, restrictions on exports may benefit consumers by lowering the domestic price of the restricted good, while reducing income for producers.[10] These trade restrictive measures usually have a net welfare-reducing effect. Recent evidence from Africa shows that NTMs have increased poverty owing to higher domestic prices (Cadot and Gourdon 2012; Kelleher and Reyes 2014; Treichel et al. 2012).

Unlike demand shocks in trading partners and changes in market access, referred to as (1) and (2) above, domestic trade policy is likely to have ambiguous effects on conflict, as it affects different groups of people in opposing ways. The impact of these policies on the probability of conflict will depend on the relative power and voice of these groups. For example, in the case of trade in food products in developing countries, a distinction is typically made between urban dwellers who are net consumers of food, and rural dwellers who are net producers of food. The urban group is usually more able to organize and to voice its concern than the rural group. Therefore, governments tend to implement policies, including trade policies, which favor urban dwellers (Lipton 1977).[11] There is very little systematic evidence on the impact of such policies on conflict. One exception is Bhavnani and Jha (2011), who examine the role of Britain's trade policy in the Quit India rebellion of 1942. They find that residents of districts in British India that were negatively affected by the policy favoring British manufactures over Indian producers were more likely to engage in violent insurrection.

By influencing trade, trade facilitation policies, such as the strengthening of transport infrastructure and the streamlining of border procedures, can also potentially affect conflict via the same mechanisms described above. These policies typically reduce the cost of trading between countries, with similar effects on trade as other policy changes. This reduction in cost could in turn increase both imports and exports. The evidence suggests that trade facilitation, including both hard and soft infrastructure, can have important effects on exports (Portugal-Perez and Wilson 2012). For fragile countries there may be a particular large scope for improvement given the large gaps in trade facilitation indicators in these countries documented above. If the change in exports is large enough, this could generate employment and income opportunities, which may reduce the willingness of the population to engage in political violence. Similarly, the increase in imports would have the same effects as an import increase spurred by a reduction of trade protection.

Trading with Neighbors

Modern civil conflicts often involve substantial foreign participation, an aspect that is not often highlighted in the economics literature. Gersovitz and Kriger (2013) argue that almost all recent, major civil conflicts in Africa are more properly viewed as part of a "regional war complex" than as purely domestic conflicts.[12] The authors provide many examples of foreign participation in civil conflicts, such as the role of Côte d'Ivoire in Taylor's invasion of Liberia in 1989, which generated the Liberian civil war, and the role of South Africa and Zimbabwe in the conflict between Renamo and Frelimo in Mozambique. Consistent with this evidence, Gleditsch (2007) finds that the transnational linkages between a country and regional countries strongly influence the risk of civil conflict. Within the regional context, it is predominantly the neighboring countries that exert an influence on domestic civil conflicts (Buhaug and Gleditsch 2008).

It is thus likely that trade with neighboring countries can play an important role in civil conflicts. A high volume of trade between two neighbors A and B increases the costs to A of a conflict in B, thus reducing the likelihood that A would intervene to foment civil conflict in B (and vice versa).[13] Trade may also raise the level of trust between groups in different countries (Rohner, Thoenig, and Zilibotti 2013), for example because trade relations may require learning the language or the customs of the other group, thus reducing the likelihood of interventions in support of civil conflicts.[14] Gleditsch (2007) finds that greater trade integration with a country's neighbors substantially reduces the risk of civil war in that country.[15]

This result, while preliminary, underlines the importance of trade integration between neighbors, especially in more fragile contexts. Improved trade facilitation and trade agreements with neighboring countries could help reduce the risk of civil conflict. This is one of the rationales behind the trade integration programs funded by the World Bank in the Great Lakes region, an area ridden with long-standing regional conflicts.

Cross-Country Evidence on Trade Shocks and Conflict

We offer two different approaches to testing some of the theoretical hypotheses that emerge above. This section considers whether a relationship between changes in trade and the onset, duration, or intensity of conflict can be identified across countries. The next two sections present evidence on this relationship from two country studies, on Nigeria and the Israeli-Palestinian conflict in the West Bank and Gaza. Each of these analyses covers some, but not all, of the trade-related changes that may affect conflict. The cross-country analysis considers imported and exported commodity prices, changes in economic conditions in major trading partners, and trading with neighbors; the Nigerian case tests for the impact of changes in the prices of produced commodities and changes in the prices of consumed goods; and the Palestinian case focuses on the changes in trading conditions with the major trading partner. Our empirical work builds on the young, but growing literature on estimating the relationship between changes in income and civil conflict, while attempting to address some of the methodological issues raised by these studies (box 1.2).

Box 1.2 Empirical Issues in the Early Literature on the Relationship between Changes in Income and Conflict

Earlier empirical studies, such as Collier and Hoeffler (1998, 2004) and Fearon and Laitin (2003), find support for a negative relationship between income levels and shocks on one side, and coups, violence, and war on the other. However, the interpretation of these findings differs. Collier and Hoeffler (2004) interpret the negative relationship as a confirmation of the opportunity cost hypothesis, namely that the cost of recruiting rebels increases with income growth. Fearon and Laitin (2003) argue that the result is instead driven by the strong positive association between state capacity and income. When income is low, the state's ability to contain possible rebellions is limited.

While these papers have been influential, their cross-country empirical work suffers from a number of drawbacks (Blattman and Miguel 2010). Importantly, these studies do not fully account for how the relationship between income and conflict varies, depending on country circumstances (called heterogeneity). Nor do these studies address the likelihood that changes in income and conflict are interdependent rather than causation running only from income changes to conflict (referred to as endogneity), which can distort empirical estimates.

The subsequent literature has tried to address these limitations. In an analysis of the impact of income changes on conflict in sub-Saharan Africa, Miguel, Satyanath, and Sergenti (2004) take into account much of the heterogeneity by controlling for differences among countries that do not vary over time, but may be important in determining the relationship between changes in income and conflict.[a] To deal with endogeneity, they isolate the portion of income changes that is explained by rainfall variation, which is not affected by the conflict. Their analysis confirms a significant negative effect of income on the incidence of conflict. Since changes in income in Africa are mainly related to labor-intensive agriculture, this result lends support to the opportunity cost hypothesis.

This work helped trigger an interest in the use of weather shocks as an instrument for income changes or as a direct determinant of conflict. Studies almost invariably find that large deviations from normal weather patterns increase the probability of conflict (Hsiang and Burke 2013). This finding is particularly clear in sub-Saharan Africa. Using small geographic cells as the unit of analysis, Harari and La Ferrara (2012) show that negative climate changes affect conflict incidence in Africa only during the growing season. This is consistent with the effect channeled via changes in income.[b]

a. More formally, they use a fixed effects model.
b. This finding is also shared by within-country studies on the determinants of conflict at the local level in Somalia (Maystadt and Ecker 2014), Brazil (Hidalgo et al. 2010), and India (Gawande 2012). And it also applies to cross-country studies using different kinds of changes that affect incomes, for example the movements in foreign interest rates in relevant partner countries used in Hull and Imai (2013).

Empirical Results on Trade and Conflict Onset

Our main empirical analysis estimates the impact of various trade-related variables on the onset of conflict. We use the dataset prepared by the Uppsala Conflict Data Programme (referred to as the PRIO dataset), and include all examples of conflict with battle deaths above 25 per year, not just major conflicts (see appendix A). The onset of conflict is viewed as a function of: 1) the export price index; 2) the import price index; 3) an indicator of changes in the demand of major trading partners; 4) the share of trade with neighbors in a country's total trade; 5) a set of control variables that vary over time, including the presence of conflict since 1946, the incidence of conflict in neighboring countries and in some specifications a coup attempt in the year before; 6) a comprehensive set of variables that do not vary over time and may influence the probability of conflict, such as geography, ethnicity, religion, and colonial history; 7) a set of variables controlling for any variation over time common to all countries; 8) countries' time trends; and 9) an error term. Appendix B provides a more formal description of the model and estimation techniques used, along with the tables showing the estimation results (table B.1 presents the results for our preferred specification of the model, discussed immediately below).

We find that the *export price index* is positively and significantly associated with the onset of conflict. We test both contemporaneous and lagged increases in prices, with the positive relationship mainly driven by the contemporaneous variable. A one standard deviation increase in the export price index raises the probability of conflict by 4 percent in the same year.[16] The signs of the lagged coefficients are consistent with the negative autocorrelation of commodity prices (i.e. the coefficient on the export price index in $t-1$ is negative and that on $t-2$ is positive). Importantly, the sum of the three coefficients for the export price index (the contemporaneous coefficient and two lags) is positive and significant. It suggests that an increase of 10 percent in the export price index raises the risk of conflict by 2.2 percentage points.

The positive and significant effect of the export price index on conflict contradicts the finding in the similar analysis of Bazzi and Blattman (2014), where the coefficient on the commodity price index was not significant.[17] As the estimation strategy and the data are comparable, this difference has to do with the different way the price index is computed. Bazzi and Blattman (2014) use the change in the price index, while we use the level of the price index. Indeed when we compute the coefficient on the change in the price index, its contemporaneous coefficient becomes less significant and the sum of the contemporaneous and lagged coefficients becomes not significant, as in Bazzi and Blattman (2014).

There is good reason to believe that it is the price level rather than its proportionate change over the previous period that matters most in shaping the incentives to engage in violence. Consider for instance a change in the price of oil for an oil-exporting country. During periods of low international prices, even a large percentage change in price in one period may be associated with a low price level at the end of the period. In this case, the value of the oil vulnerable to predation would still be limited, thus keeping the incentives for fighting over its control relatively low.[18] We therefore believe that our price index is more suited to capture changes in the incentives to engage in conflict due to commodity price changes. This approach is also in line with other recent studies, for example Nunn and Qian (2014) and Dube and Vargas (2013).

We argue that the positive relation between the export price index and conflict onset can also in part explain the timing of the recent civil war in Republic of South Sudan (box 1.3).

As expected, the estimated relationship between conflict and the *import price index* is positive: higher import prices reduce real incomes, thus reducing the opportunity cost of conflict. However, the coefficient is not statistically significant. This finding differs from the significant, positive impact found by Arezki

---

Box 1.3 The South Sudanese Civil War: Was Oil Export the Trigger?

Republic of South Sudan obtained its independence in 2011 after long years of fighting against Sudan, which culminated in a UN-supervised popular referendum. The country has experienced a very tormented period since independence. After a war with Sudan in 2012 in the oil rich regions on the border, it descended into civil war in December 2013. The dispute started following the sacking of the vice-president Riek Machar by the president Salva Kiir, both members of the Sudan People's Liberation Movement (S.P.L.M.) but long-standing political opponents. This move accelerated the collapse of the fragile government's balance of power established also along ethnic lines (Kiir belongs to the Dinka, the country's largest ethnic group, while Machar belongs to the second largest group, the Nuer). The fighting erupted in the capital Juba with an alleged coup attempt led by Machar but has since extended to much of the country, especially in the oil-producing regions of the north. By early January 2014 the violence had caused over 10,000 deaths and hundreds of thousands of internally displaced people.

The political roots of the war are clear, reflecting the unsuccessful state-building process so far and the divisions within the S.P.L.M. However, the triggers behind the war's outbreak are less clear. What triggered the political crisis in July after two years since independence in which the divisions of power within the government and the party had been fairly stable?

One possible explanation, which fits with the findings in this report, is the "rapacity effect." The political divisions between Kiir and Machar became salient again once oil exports to Sudan resumed in April 2013. At that point the value of the unchecked control over the state, whose fiscal revenues depend entirely on the oil exports, increased dramatically. Given the absence of any transparency and accountability (there is not even a regular public disclosure of the actual petroleum sales), this control is particularly appealing in Republic of South Sudan with the government enjoying complete discretion over the management of the oil revenues. Indeed, accusations of embezzlement of public funds from oil revenues have been frequent at the highest political level.[a] By sacking Machar, Kiir ensured that the control of these revenues would not have to be shared with his political opponent and his faction.

box continues next page

Box 1.3 The South Sudanese Civil War: Was Oil Export the Trigger? *(continued)*

A comparison with another oil dependent country in post-independence transition, Timor-Leste, lends credit to this hypothesis. The country achieved independence in 2002. Its transition has also been marred by some violence in May–June 2006 (though not on the scale of that in Republic of South Sudan), but this does not seem related to the swings in oil revenues. Since Timor-Leste's independence oil exports have continued to grow and even the discovery of the large Bayu-Undan oil and gas field in 2004 did not disrupt the political context.

Why haven't changes in oil exports triggered instability in Timor-Leste? One important difference with Republic of South Sudan is the transparent way in which the oil revenues are managed in Timor-Leste, which reduces the government discretion over the spending of the revenues. The Revenue Watch Institute (2013) rates Timor-Leste among the top and Republic of South Sudan among the lowest countries in terms of the quality of governance in the oil, gas, and mining sector. This high quality (unprecedented among fragile countries) was achieved also through the set up—with the World Bank assistance—of a sovereign wealth fund in 2005 to manage most of the oil revenues in a way to maximize transparency and accountability. The fund is structured through a bank account abroad, which can be accessed only through parliament approval. To bolster transparency, Timor-Leste was also one of the first countries to join the Extractive Industries Transparency Initiative (EITI). As argued by the Independent Evaluation Group (2011), this regime has set new standards for developing countries in regard to transparency and accountability in the management of petroleum revenues, and in limiting their arbitrary use.

a. The South Sudanese auditor-general noted that over $1 billion from oil revenues was already unaccounted for before independence (in 2005–06), and in 2012 Salva Kiir accused senior officials of stealing over $4 billion in state funds (Al Jazeera 2012). At the onset of the civil conflict in December 2013, Riek Machar accused Salva Kiir and his government of embezzling $4.5 billion (Wudu 2013).

and Bruckner (2011). On the other hand, this finding is consistent with the note of caution highlighted above, i.e. a developing country's commodity imports account for only a limited share of total consumption of commodities, since a large share of consumption, especially among poorer households, comes from domestic production (Bazzi and Blattman 2014).

The estimated relationship between conflict and changes in the *markets of major trading partners* is negative, consistent with the idea that increases in demand from trading partners increases real incomes, thus increasing the opportunity cost of conflict. However, this relationship is also not significantly different from zero, according to standard statistical tests. This suggests that the economic cycles in the export destination markets do not affect the probability of conflict at home, unlike other economic shocks such as rainfall (Miguel, Satyanath, and Sergenti 2004) and foreign interest rate movements (Hull and Imai 2013).[19]

Trade with neighbors is not found to have a significant impact on conflict. One reason may be that a country may attempt to foster trade with neighboring countries that are potential sources of instability. Thus estimates of the relationship between trade with neighbors and conflict may find it difficult to distinguish between the tendency for trade to reduce conflict and the choice of trading partners that are inherently more likely to foment conflict.

Some evidence for this issue can be seen in the growth of regional trade agreements (RTAs) during the second half of the 20th century, where the desire to nurture peaceful relations with neighbors was an important motivation (Martin, Mayer, and Thoenig 2012). While the authors focus on inter-state conflicts, the same argument may also apply to domestic civil conflicts, as many such conflicts are fuelled by foreign countries, especially in the same region (Gersovitz and Kriger 2013). This argument suggests that a country may sign RTAs with the goal of improving relationships with countries that otherwise could be a source of instability. In the extreme, only those neighbors of a country X with which X has signed an RTA may be important in destabilizing X. Some insight into this issue can be gained by testing the relationship between the likelihood of conflict and the share of trade with neighbors with which a country has signed an RTA.[20] This variable has a negative and significant association with the onset of conflict.[21] However, the estimation of this relationship is difficult, given the likely two-way causation between conflict and the signing of RTAs (box 1.4).

Mixed results are obtained for the *time-varying control variables*. Having had a past conflict (since 1946) raises the probability of conflict by 18 percent, which confirms the findings in World Bank (2011). On the other hand, neither the

---

Box 1.4 Correcting for Endogeneity When Measuring the Relationship between Conflict and Trade under RTAs

We find that trade with neighbors with which a country has signed an RTA is negatively associated with the onset of conflict. One problem with this approach is that our trade under RTAs variable may violate an important assumption of this kind of empirical test, namely that the independent variables (in this case, trade under RTAs) are not caused by the dependent variable (conflict). Indeed, this endogeneity problem likely exists, since part of the driver behind RTAs could be the desire of intensifying the economic relations with neighbors that may otherwise be able to destabilize the country (similarly to the Martin, Mayer, and Thoenig 2012 story for inter-state wars).

We attempt to correct for this issue by introducing a less endogenous representative of our trade under RTAs variable, namely trade under RTAs that have been entered into by more than two countries (so that strategic motives of reducing tensions may be less important). Using this variable generates similar results as before, since it is highly correlated with the trade under RTAs variable. The coefficients are only slightly more negative and significant, providing some evidence that, if anything, the endogeneity biases the absolute size of the coefficients downwards.

This instrument is not likely to fully address the endogeneity issue, and in the absence of a suitable instrument, we can only interpret this result as suggestive evidence of the importance of promoting trade via formal agreements with contiguous countries in order to prevent civil conflict. Future research would need to test this hypothesis more thoroughly.

---

presence of a major conflict in the neighboring countries, nor a coup attempt the year before, significantly affects the conflict probability in the country of interest.

Qualifications and Alternative Tests

In the above results, a conflict is defined as those with more than 25 battle deaths per year. Another approach would be to perform the same empirical test but consider only major conflicts, or those with more than 1,000 battle deaths per year. However, the results are considerably weaker than when considering all conflicts. The effect of the export price index on major conflicts is not significantly different from zero overall, although its lagged coefficient is negative and significant (see last four columns of table B.1). The results for the import price index, changes in the markets of major trading partners, and trade with neighbors are also not significant.

Taken at their face value, these results suggest that changes in exports affect the eruption of minor conflicts but not of major civil wars. That would be the case, for instance, if these shocks influence local conflicts, which do not eventually spill into large-scale civil wars. That would be consistent with evidence from Colombia (Dube and Vargas 2013) and the Democratic Republic of Congo (Maystadt et al. 2013). However, the lack of significance of the results for major conflicts could also be a product of the "rare event" bias. This refers to the difficulty in identifying a significant relationship when the dependent variable has a large number of zeroes (King and Zeng 2001). This problem is more likely to occur when the dependent variable includes only major conflicts, as this is a much rarer event than minor conflicts. We therefore consider the specifications that define conflicts as more than 25 battle deaths a year as our preferred ones.

These results are robust to a wide array of checks. Adding country-specific time trends and adopting a different approach to calculating the price indices generate very similar results to those described above (see table B.2).

One possible issue is that our results assume that the export price index is not affected by developments in the country experiencing conflict (otherwise the coefficient on the export price index will not be estimated correctly). This is appropriate for most developing countries, which are typically price takers in international commodity markets. However, some countries do account for a significant share of the market for their main export product.

We use two strategies to deal with this concern. First, we exclude from country X's export basket the commodities for which X's share in world exports is above a certain threshold (10 percent in column 1 and 20 percent in column 3 of table B.3), and obtain results that are similar to our baseline results. The main difference is that the coefficient of the export price index is smaller, but still significant at the 10 percent threshold. Second, we exclude the countries that are large exporters of at least one commodity (in one year) according to the 10 percent or 20 percent criterion. This approach has the advantage of not generating artificial biases in the countries' export baskets. However, this approach also leads to a reduced sample that may be less representative than the full sample of developing countries as a group. The results are the same as in our baseline results.

Finally, we test whether our results are different if we use an alternative source (prepared by the Correlates of War Project—COW) for the conflict data.[22] While we feel that the PRIO data is more reliable, it is reassuring that the main results do not vary much across datasets. The comparison—reported in columns 5–6 of table B.3—shows that the individual trade variables' coefficients are not significantly different across the datasets. The only exception is that contemporaneous coefficient on the import price index is positive and significant in COW and negative but not significant in PRIO. However, the sum of the cotemporaneous and lagged import price index variables is not significant with either dataset, a result in line with that obtained earlier using the same high threshold for defining civil conflicts.

Differentiating between Commodities

As discussed above, the impact of commodity prices on conflict differ along two dimensions: 1) whether they are point-source or diffused commodities; and 2) whether they are consumed domestically or not. Testing the first distinction reveals that the positive impact of the export price index on conflict (shown above) is mainly due to point-source commodities. By contrast, the effect of diffused commodities on the probability of conflict is not significant (column 1 of table B.4 in appendix B).[23] These results are consistent with the rapacity effect, while they provide no support to the opportunity cost effect.

For the second distinction, only commodities that are consumed domestically have a positive and significant impact on conflict onset (although the coefficient on the price index of commodities that are not consumed domestically also has a positive sign). This result appears consistent with the expectation that increases in the prices of commodities that are consumed domestically reduce the opportunity cost of engaging in conflict. However, further analysis indicates that the result may be driven by the domestically consumed, point-source commodities (e.g. oil and gas), and not domestically consumed, diffuse commodities (e.g. food). Thus the estimated positive relationship between conflict and domestically consumed commodities may reflect the rapacity effect, or the competition for point-source commodities, rather than the impact of rising prices on the real incomes of consumers.

Further evidence, albeit only partial, can be seen by splitting the export price index into the four types of commodities that combine the two dimensions as in table 1.2 (see column 3 of table B.4). While the coefficients of the sub-indices are not significant, the magnitudes suggest that point-source, consumed commodities exert the largest impact on conflict of all the subcategories. This group comprises oil and gas, which represent important consumption items in many developing countries, especially in the urban areas. In the absence of consumption data by country, it is not possible to disentangle the rapacity effect from the consumption effect in this case. Noting that our variable is constructed on the basis of the export shares, we interpret this mainly as a rapacity effect.

The coefficients of the diffuse export commodities are also not significantly different from zero for both the consumed (which has a negative sign) and the non-consumed (which has a positive sign).

This result confirms the lack of support for the opportunity cost effect, at least via the export sector. Even the commodity group that should provide the cleanest test for the opportunity cost effect—i.e. diffused, not consumed commodities—does not have a significant relationship with conflict. On the other hand, the weakly positive sign suggests that some form of resource effect may be at work even with diffused commodities, for example as the revenues from these commodities may also be taxed by rebel groups to fund their struggle.

Impact on Conflict Ending or Intensity

So far the dependent variable has been the onset of conflict. It is also useful to test the impact of the same trade variables on the probability of a conflict ending and the intensity of conflict (equation 6 in appendix A). The results for conflict ending (given in columns 1–4 in table B.5) are difficult to interpret. The relationship between the export price index and conflict ending is not significant (while it was significant when testing its impact on conflict onset), while the relationship between trade with neighbors and conflict ending is positive and significant (while it was not significant with conflict onset). In line with the previous results, the trade variables do not have a significant impact on the probability of a conflict ending when considering only major conflicts (columns 5–8 in table B.5).[24] These results suggest that the trade variables we have examined do not seem to matter much in affecting the duration of an ongoing conflict.

More interesting results are obtained in testing the impact of the trade variables on conflict intensity (the dependent variable is the number of battle deaths). Both the export price index and import price index have a positive and significant impact on conflict intensity, which is consistent with the rapacity and opportunity cost effects, respectively (column 1 of table B.6). However, for the export price index the conflict-inducing effect is actually driven by diffused rather than by point-source commodities (column 2).[25] This is the opposite result to that on conflict onset and may suggest that ongoing conflicts are intensified by increases in the price of diffused exported commodities. While this finding is different from that in Bazzi and Blattman (2014), who find a weak effect of export prices on conflict intensity, it is consistent with the idea that production of diffused commodities may provide an important source of revenues for rebel groups to fund their struggle, thus intensifying existing conflicts.

The extent to which rebel groups may support their activities through taxing diffused commodities varies across contexts as well as across commodities. For example, a rise in coca production fostered violence in Colombia by raising the guerrilla's revenues (Angrist and Kugler 2008). Similarly, the cross-country evidence provided by Nunn and Qian (2014) is consistent with small armed groups using U.S. food aid to fund local conflicts. On the other hand, Dube and Vargas (2013) find that increases in the value of production of diffused commodities reduce conflict intensity in Colombia. It is beyond the scope of this work to identify the conditions under which one or the other channel may prevail, but it is important to acknowledge that the impact of diffused commodities on conflict may be more complex than what is suggested by the simple opportunity cost theory.

Higher income growth in a country's export markets reduces the intensity of conflict. This raises two possible differences with the earlier results. First, this variable had no significant impact on the onset of conflict, suggesting that such shocks affect the intensity, but not the onset, of civil conflicts (as in Chaudion, Peskowitz, and Stanton 2012). This confirms the finding in Bazzi and Blattman (2014) that escalating an existing conflict seems easier than triggering a new one.

Second, the negative relationship between growth in a country's export markets and conflict is consistent with the opportunity cost theory. However, our finding that diffused commodities have no significant relationship with conflict onset (see above) appears to contradict the opportunity cost theory. Examining the source of this difference is beyond the scope of this analysis, but we can put forward a possible hypothesis. The relationship between conflict and the prices of diffused commodities is not significant because increases in these prices both increase the opportunity cost of conflict (thus tending to reduce conflict) and in some cases provided funding for rebel groups (thus increasing conflict). The latter effect, however, applies almost exclusively to goods produced in rural areas, as rebel groups' ability to tax local economic activity is mostly limited to rural areas. By contrast, increases in a country's export markets likely have little effect on commodity prices, which are set in international markets, but will affect demand for manufactures, whose trade is more based on importer-exporter networks and thus more affected by country-specific demand shocks.[26] Moreover, we control for commodity price shocks, reinforcing the idea that the effect of changes in export markets operates through demand for manufactures. Since manufactures production in developing countries is located mainly in urban and peri-urban areas, changes in a country's export markets are unlikely to provide rebels with additional revenues. Therefore this "rebel funding" channel could explain the relation between diffused commodity export price shocks and conflict intensity, but is less likely to apply in the case of demand shocks in export markets.

Finally, a higher share of trade with neighboring countries is significantly associated with lower conflict intensity. This finding is consistent with the idea that country X's trade with its neighbors increases their opportunity cost of destabilizing X, for example by supporting rebel groups in X.[27] While the coefficient for the impact of regional trade on conflict onset was also negative, it was not statistically significant.

Evidence from Nigerian States (2004–13)

Case studies that examine the impact of changes in trade on conflict across regions within a single country are a necessary complement to cross-country analysis. One sacrifices the opportunity to reach conclusions on conflict from a global perspective, and to gain insight on how trade affects conflicts in many different contexts. On the other hand, differences among regions, for example in political conditions and the business environment, tend to be smaller than differences among countries. Thus within-country analysis can more easily control for different conditions that may affect the relationship between trade flows and conflict. In addition, data for a single country are usually richer than across countries (e.g. on consumption and on employment), thus enabling more precise tests of effects than in cross-country analyses. This section considers the example of how changes in trade have affected the conflict in Nigeria, while the next section examines the Israeli-Palestinian conflict.

Nigeria's Civil Conflict in the Past Decade

Although it is not officially considered fragile according to the World Bank and the regional development banks, Nigeria has had a recent history of acute conflict-related violence. According to the Armed Conflict Location and Events Dataset (ACLED), from 2003 to 2013 Nigeria was the third most violent African country and suffered the fourth-highest deaths from conflict. While the country has not experienced a full-blown civil war and the state's monopoly of force does not appear to be challenged, local conflicts have been a major constraint on the country's development over the past few decades.

The form and intensity of violence has varied substantially, both across space and over time. Conflict in Nigeria is highly regionalized. Both the dominant type of violence (battles, protests, riots, and violence against civilians) and the underlying determinants of conflict differ across regions. In the past decade, four "geographies of conflict" can be identified: the North, the Niger Delta, the Middle Belt, and the urban areas. These conflicts have important common underlying traits, rooted in dysfunctional public institutions and social and economic marginalization (Joab-Peterside et al. 2012). However, the regional contexts have also played a fundamental role in shaping the particular forms and dynamics of violent conflict in each case.

In the past decade, violence in the so-called middle belt, and particularly in Plateau State, has been mainly in the form of communal violence. While much of the recent violence has occurred between Muslim and Christian communities (though some violence also has occurred within Muslim communities), unequal access to land appears to be a core driver of the conflict in the middle belt.[28] In Kwara State, for instance, the conflicts in Offa/Erin Ile can be attributed to disputes over land ownership and grazing rights.[29] In other states, minor disputes have escalated owing to improper handling. One example is the conflict in Ekiti State over the permanent site of a social amenity within the neighboring towns of Ise and Emure Ekiti.

Violence has increased since 2010 (map 1.1), particularly in the northeastern parts of the country, in large part due to the activities of the Islamic militant group Boko Haram. Indeed, the government declared a state of emergency in the three most northeastern states of Borno, Yobe, and Adamawa in May 2013. These areas also experienced some of the greatest intensification in conflict in the country, in terms of both the number of conflict events (map 1.2) and the number

Map 1.1 The Geography of Conflict in Nigeria (2004–13)

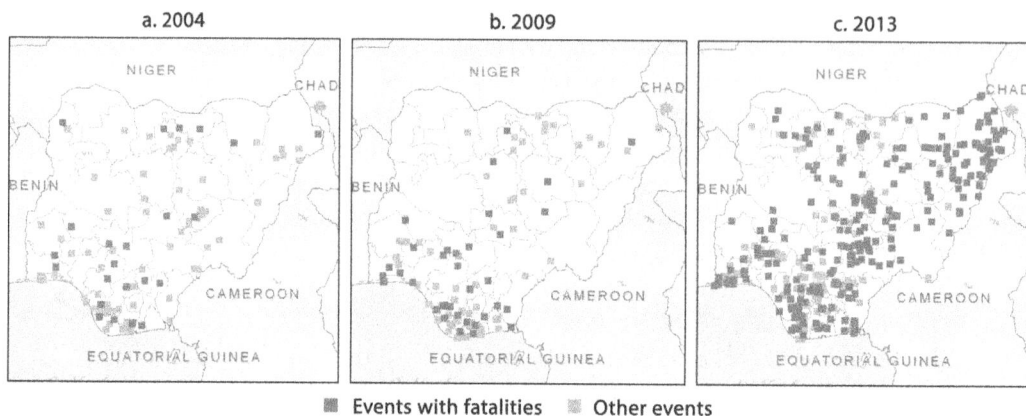

a. 2004   b. 2009   c. 2013

◼ Events with fatalities   ▦ Other events

Source: ACLED.
Note: Conflict events are all events recorded by ACLED that involve any form of political violence (i.e., battles, protests/riots, and violence against civilians).

Map 1.2 Conflict Intensity across States in Nigeria

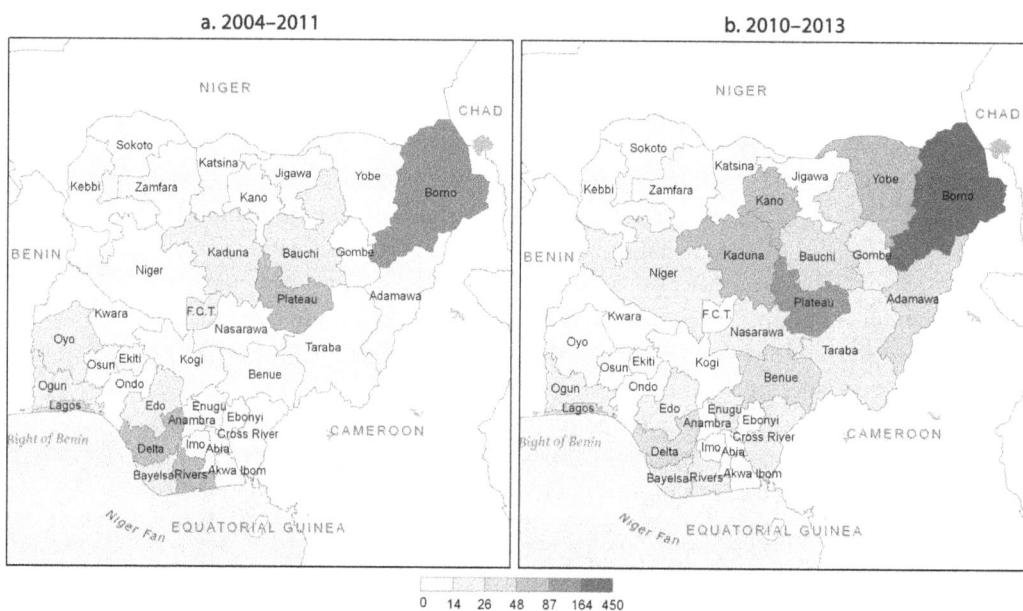

a. 2004–2011   b. 2010–2013

0   14   26   48   87   164   450

Source: ACLED.
Note: Conflict events are all events recorded by ACLED that involve any form of political violence (i.e., battles, protests/riots, and violence against civilians). The darker the color the higher the number of (any) conflict events in the period.

of fatalities (map 1.3). However, other parts of the country, particularly the middle belt states of Platteau, Kanu, and Kaduna, have also recently experienced an intensification of long-standing conflicts.

In addition, political demonstrations (particularly concerning fuel subsidies and corruption) have increased in recent years, mainly in urban areas, and have

Map 1.3 Violence Intensity across States in Nigeria

a. 2004–2011   b. 2010–2013

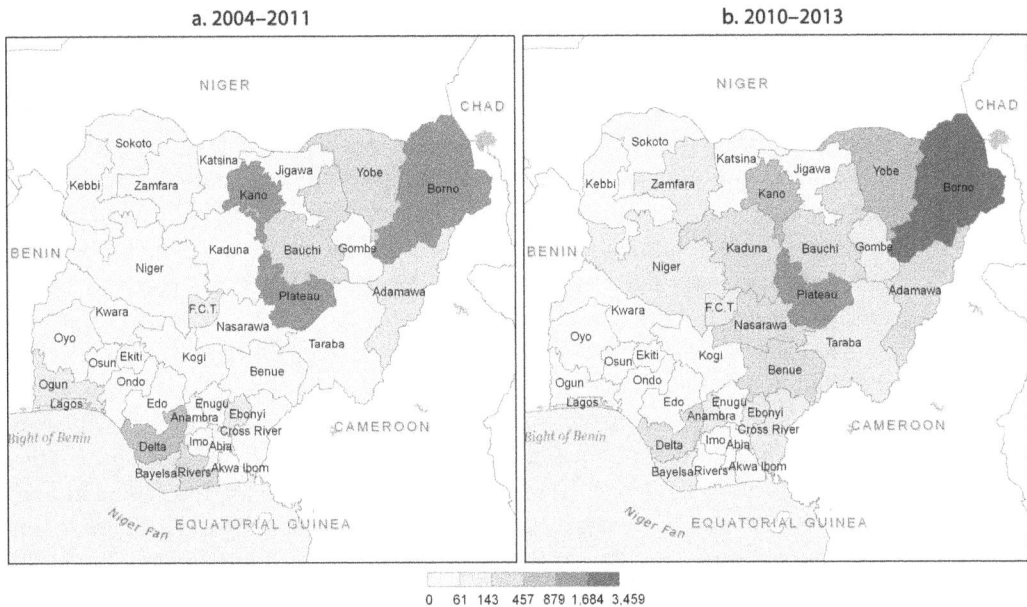

0   61   143   457 879 1,684 3,459

Source: ACLED.
Note: The darker the color the higher the number of fatalities in the period.

expressed themselves in violence. In Abuja and Lagos, over 40 percent of conflict activity is made up of rioting or protesting. Over the course of the period covered by the dataset (1997–2013), over one-third of riot and protest events have involved violence (ACLED 2013).

At the same time, conflict in other areas of the country has subsided. In particular, violence by the rebel groups in the Niger Delta states, which was among the most violent parts of the country in the 2000s, was significantly reduced after the agreement of 2009, whereby the state provided amnesty for local militants along with a disarmament, demobilization, rehabilitation and reintegration (DDRR) program. Under the amnesty, which ran from August to October 2009, militants who handed in their weapons were pardoned for their crimes, trained in nonviolence, and offered vocational training in various activities in Nigeria or overseas. After attending nonviolence training they were paid US$410 per month until they found work. Just over 26,000 young militants took the amnesty package (IRIN 2011b). While this agreement has been criticized for failing to treat the root causes of conflict, and for promoting "warlordism," it seems to have gone a long way toward reducing conflict in the short run (Sayne 2013).

Model and Data

Our basic model measures the impact on conflict across states over the period 2004–11 (as measured by the number of conflict episodes, the number of violent episodes, and the number of conflict-related fatalities) of price indices for goods produced by households, goods consumed by households, and oil. We control for various other determinants of conflict at the state level, including the size and density of the population at the beginning of the period, past incidence of various types of conflict, the poverty gap and share of the population under the poverty line at the beginning of the period, and three indicators of the potential for ethnic tensions (whether the president's ethnicity is the same as that of the dominant group in a state, whether there are at least two significant ethnic minority groups, and whether there is more than one dominant ethnic group). In addition we control for all possible time varying covariates of conflict at the regional level (for each of the six macro-regions in Nigeria).

The data on conflict are from the Armed Conflict Location and Event Data Project (ACLED), which records individual conflict events from media sources, allowing for the construction of statewide measures of conflict intensity over time. The price indices are based on urban prices reported by Nigeria's National Bureau of Statistics (NBS), which collects monthly data for 143 food and non-food items by state. In the consumer price index, the state-level NBS prices are weighted by the share of each good in household consumption. Similarly, in the producer price index, the NBS prices are weighted by the share of each good in household production. Data on production and consumption behavior are taken from household surveys. The oil price index is calculated by multiplying the value of oil production in 2003 by the international oil price. A more formal explanation of how these indices are calculated, and an explanation of the several choices required to deal with data issues (e.g. the use of urban and not rural data on prices, how the NBS price data are matched to survey data on goods produced and consumed by households, and the calculation of oil production at the state level) is provided in appendix A.

While our goal is to estimate the impact on conflict of our two price indices (of household production and consumption goods), it is equally true that conflict will affect these price indices. For instance, high levels of conflict may reduce local production, and if markets are imperfectly integrated across space, this may boost local prices. Conflict may also reduce local demand, which would have an opposite effect on prices. This endogeneity would bias the relationship between the price indices and conflict. Typically, this endogeneity problem is corrected for by using an independent variable (called an *instrument*) that is similar to the independent variable of interest, but not affected by the dependent variable. Many studies (e.g. Bazzi and Blattman 2014; Dube and Vargas 2013) use international prices as instruments for domestic prices. However, this does not work very well in our study, because international prices are available only for internationally traded commodities, which often do not include many local products important for consumption and production in Nigeria (e.g. yam and cassava). Moreover, international prices do not account for the price transmission from international to domestic markets, which is often limited. Thus international prices may not provide an ideal representation of the size of the change in price at the local level, and thus have only a weak relationship with conflict. However, the international price indices are useful for checking the robustness of the results. In addition (unlike the domestic price indices) they are available through 2013.

Our main specification uses instruments that are constructed on the basis of domestic prices of faraway states, following the same logic of Jacoby (2013) for changes in rice prices in Indian districts. The price data for the other Nigerian states should reflect exogenous international price changes, their transmission to the domestic market, and shifts in demand and supply in the large domestic markets outside of the particular state in question. We exclude neighboring states that may be affected by the conditions in the state in question, to ensure that they are not affected by conflict within that state. A formal presentation of how these various price indices are constructed and of the method of derivation of exogenous prices indices is given in appendix A.

Results

In our preferred specification, the relationship between the producer price index (calculated with prices of faraway states) and conflict is negative and statistically significant.[30] A 10 percent increase in the producer price index will lead to a reduction of 2.3 conflict events (column 3 of table B.10), while holding all other variables in the model constant. The relationship between the consumer price index (again calculated with the prices of faraway states) and conflict is positive, statistically significant, and slightly larger than that of the producer price index. These results provide substantial evidence that changes in real incomes affect conflict by changing the opportunity cost of participating in violence: as real incomes rise (both through increases in producer prices and declines in consumer prices), the incidence of conflict falls, and vice versa.

This result is consistent with that from an alternative specification which excludes the consumer price index. In this case, the producer price index has no statistically significant impact on conflict. This suggests that failure to include this consumption impact severely biases (toward zero) the conflict-reducing effect of increases in prices of agricultural commodities produced by the households. The issue here is that the prices used in construction of the producer price index involve goods that are both consumed in, and produced by, households. Thus increases in the producer price index may raise real incomes (and thus the opportunity cost of fighting) for households that are predominantly affected through the goods they produce, and lower real incomes for households that are predominantly affected through the goods they consume. Once we control for this (positive) consumption effect through the consumer price index, we are able to isolate the true (negative) production effect of producer prices on conflict. This is an important finding, as the literature has tended to focus solely on the impact of prices of produced goods on conflict, thus potentially suffering from an important omitted variable bias. This may also help explain the lack of consensus on the effects of agricultural commodity prices on conflict.

The oil index has a positive and significant effect on the number of conflict events the following year, in line with the state prize hypothesis: exogenous increases in the value of oil raise the incentive for fighting in the production areas. However, this effect disappears after the amnesty agreement in 2009, confirming that the agreement was effective in curbing violence in the Niger Delta states. In fact, the insignificant association between the oil price index and conflict intensity after 2009 is consistent with the idea that the oil funds may have helped to demobilize militant groups in these areas (Sayne 2013). In the period up to the agreement, a 10 percent increase in the oil index only increases conflict events by 0.14. This smaller average effect (relative to the other commodities' effect) is partly due to the fact that it only applies to a few states and partly to the fact that the oil price index varies more than the producer and consumer price indices.

While we do not report the coefficients of the control variables (full results are available upon request), an interesting result is that the ethnicity of the president matters in determining the level of conflict in each state. When the president's ethnicity is the same as that of the dominant group in a state, conflict intensity subsides, confirming the importance of ethnic allegiance in state politics. This result is weaker for those states with more than one dominant ethnic group.

These results are robust to various tests. If we use contemporaneous (rather than lagged) values of the price indices, the consumption and oil price indices are still significant, but the production price index and the oil price index (after 2009) are not. The weak result for the contemporaneous producer price index implies that the impact of price changes on conflict occurs with a lag (even the significant result for the contemporaneous consumption price index is weaker than with its lagged value).[31] Similar results are found if we include both the contemporaneous and lagged values of the price indices.[32] The results are also robust to the inclusion of the lagged unemployment rate as a further control, which, however, makes the producer price coefficient less significant (column 3 of table B.11).

We also test for using international prices to calculate the producer and consumer price indices, rather than the domestic prices described above. Once again, the relationship between the consumer price index and conflict is weaker than in the preferred specification, while the relationship between the producer price and conflict is no longer significant. Comparable results are obtained when using an alternative econometric technique (the poisson estimator, see appendix B).

The results for the use of contemporaneous variables and international price indices confirm that consumption, production, and oil prices have a significant impact on conflict events, although production effects are somewhat less robust than the others.

Comparable results also are obtained using alternative measures of conflict (events that result in fatalities, battle events, protests and riots, and violence against civilians) as the dependent variable (columns 1–12 in table B.12). The consumption and oil price effect, but not the production price effect, remain significant when using the number of fatalities as the dependent variable (column 13 of table B.12).[33] This analysis also shows an important dichotomy in the effect of the price changes. While the effect of consumer and producer prices is particularly large for protests/riots, changes in oil prices have no effect on this type of conflict event (and that is the only type of conflict event that oil does not affect). This result is consistent with the view that the violence surrounding oil extraction was mainly organized around militant groups, and was unrelated to popular protests.

The Boko Haram Conflict

As noted above, the most devastating Nigerian conflict in recent years has been associated with Boko Haram. According to the International Crisis Group (2014) Boko Haram (usually translated loosely as "Western education is forbidden") emerged in the early 2000s as an Islamic movement in northern Nigeria led by the charismatic cleric Mohammed Yusuf. Its aim is to establish an Islamic state in the north with strict adherence to Sharia law as it "believes that corrupt, false Muslims control northern Nigeria" (p. i).

The clashes between the group—which wanted to change the political and religious order of the region—and the police started in 2009 and quickly escalated into an armed insurrection, which was crushed by the state forces. Hundreds of Boko Haram's members were killed and the group's principal mosque was destroyed. Yusuf was captured by the army, handed over to the police, and shortly thereafter extra-judicially executed in public (International Crisis Group 2014; Nossiter and Kirkpatrick 2014). This spurred the retaliation of Boko Haram, which went underground and a year later launched attacks on police stations and military barracks, explicitly in revenge for the killings of Yusuf and his comrades (International Crisis Group 2014).

However, the attacks continued to escalate, including attacks against civilians. As a response the Nigerian government assembled a joint task force of military and police units to battle Boko Haram and declared a "state of emergency" in three northeastern states—Borno, Yobe, and Adamawa—in May 2013. However, that has not seemed to reduce the violence, which included the murder of sixty-five students at the agricultural college in Yobe State in September 2013, chainsaw beheadings of truck drivers, and the killing of hundreds on the roads of northern Nigeria (Council on Foreign Relations 2014). Most recently the abduction of 200 schoolgirls in Borno State spurred a worldwide wave of condemnation of the group.

While the conflict has a clear religious dimension, analysts suggest that grievances, including those motivated by poverty and unemployment, are fundamental drivers of the increased militant activities of Boko Haram (International Crisis Group 2014; IRIN 2011a).[34] This type of economic grievances may have facilitated the recruitment of Boko Haram, which incentivized poor youth to join their ranks by offering food, shelter, and other forms of assistance not provided by the government (Copeland 2013).

We use the same approach as above to determine to what extent trade-related changes in income explain the surge in the Boko Haram conflict in the past few years. As we don't have state-level domestic prices after 2010, the changes in consumption and production measures are based on international prices.

The results of the analysis suggest that income shocks via both consumption and production price changes exert an important influence on the intensity of the Boko Haram conflict. The direction of the effects is consistent with that of the previous analysis, although this time the impact of production shock on conflict events is larger than consumption. On average a 10 percent reduction in the value of the production index in a year leads to 2.38 additional conflict events involving Boko Haram in the following year, while the same reduction in consumption prices leads to 0.95 fewer events (column 1 in table B.14). The effects are even larger (3.7 and 2.5 respectively for production and consumption prices) when considering only the three northern regions where Boko Haram activities are concentrated: production (column 2 in table B.14). These results are even more striking, considering that the data on international prices may not reflect accurately local market conditions as argued above. On the other hand, the oil index does not bear any significant relation with Boko Haram conflict activities.

Interestingly, neither consumption nor production price indices appear to be associated with non Boko Haram conflict events either in the full sample or in the northern regions (columns 3 and 4 in table B.14). This suggests that income shocks, at least driven by consumption and production price changes, appear to matter for current conflicts in Nigeria mainly through the Boko Haram insurgency. On the other hand, the oil index is associated with a reduction in non Boko Haram conflict, confirming our previous results for the post-2009 period.

The conflict inducing effects of increases in the consumption basket price carry through also for the number of violent conflict events and of fatalities while that is not the case for the prices of the production basket, which becomes insignificant. The effect of consumption prices on fatalities is substantial: a 10 percent increase in the price of the consumption basket in a state generates an additional 19 fatalities in that state.

These results confirm the view that the Boko Haram conflict has an important economic dimension, which affects the intensity of the militants' activities. They are consistent with the view that changes in incomes affect the propensity of the local populations to support the Boko Haram insurgency and/or the ability of Boko Haram to recruit fighters. This opportunity cost story seems to be even more relevant than for the other current conflicts in Nigeria.

Evidence from the Israeli-Palestinian Conflict (2000–04)

A case study of the decades-long Israeli-Palestinian conflict has an important advantage from the perspective of our model of how changes in trade affect conflict. Unlike the cross-country analysis or the Nigerian study, Palestinian exports do not include point-source commodities such as oil or minerals that might be the target of appropriation through violence. Moreover, in the cross-country analysis the possibility that rebels might use diffuse commodities to fund their activities complicated the interpretation of the estimated relationship between changes in the prices of these commodities and conflict. By contrast, the Palestinian Authority has only a limited ability to tax private earnings, thus minimizing the potential to use increased exports to curb (or to increase) violence against Israel. Eliminating the rapacity effect and the resources effect as possible interpretations of our results allows us to focus on testing the opportunity cost hypothesis. So far, tests of the opportunity cost hypothesis in studies of the Israeli-Palestinian conflict have shown mixed results (box 1.5).

Palestinian Trade Prior to the Second Intifada

Understanding the impact of changes in trade flows on the Israeli-Palestinian conflict requires understanding the degree to which Palestinian tradable production is dependent on Israel. Almost 90 percent of Palestinian merchandise exports is destined for Israel.[35] Further, Palestinian external trade is de facto regulated by Israel. Following the Oslo accords in 1993, the West Bank and Gaza and Israel have become part of a de facto custom union with a common external tariff decided by Israel, which during the 1990s controlled all the borders of the custom union, with no tariffs or quotas imposed between Israel and the West Bank and Gaza.[36] While the latter can de jure have its own trade policy, e.g. it can sign trade agreements with third parties, in reality any imports destined for the West Bank or Gaza have to enter the union via an international border controlled by Israel, which automatically charges the Israeli import tariff for goods from the specific country of origin.

Box 1.5 The Literature on the Israeli-Palestinian Conflict and the Opportunity Cost of Violence

Studies of the Israeli-Palestinian conflict have provided evidence both for and against the opportunity cost mechanism. Berrebi (2007) shows that an individual with a higher education and standard of living is more likely to become a suicide bomber (which is not consistent with the opportunity cost hypothesis), while Sayre (2009) and Saleh (2009) using district-level data find the opposite relationship. In addition, Cali, Miaari, and Fallah (2014) find no support for the opportunity cost mechanism by relating districts' public sector employment and Palestinian fatalities in the West Bank and Gaza during and after the Second Intifada. One interpretation of these latter findings is that engaging in political violence has little opportunity cost for public sector employees, as they do not face a high cost from shirking.

In a related study, Miaari, Zussman, and Zussman (2014) find that localities which were relatively more dependent on employment in Israel experienced relatively more fatalities after Israel's abrupt imposition of severe restrictions on the employment of Palestinians within its borders at the outbreak of the Second Intifada. This assumes that the large variation in the pre-Intifada employment rates in Israel across West Bank localities was unrelated to prior levels of involvement in the conflict. These results may provide some prima facie support for the opportunity cost mechanism for private employees. Our analysis will take this channel into account by including the localities' share of employment in Israel.

Trading Away from Conflict · http://dx.doi.org/10.1596/978-1-4648-0308-6

Moreover, Israeli control of the international borders implies that Palestinian exporters and importers have a strong incentive to use Israeli intermediaries to clear their goods. Israeli intermediaries reduce the cost and time of trading relative to those faced by Palestinian traders. Palestinian imports and exports are subject to twice the costs of Israeli imports and exports using the same port facilities in Israel (World Bank 2010). Importing procedures take on average as much as four times longer for Palestinians than for Israelis (40 days vs. 10 days). It is estimated that 58 percent of the Palestinian imports from Israel in 2008 were through trading companies, most of which was for reexport (Bank of Israel 2010).

The opening up of the Israeli import regime in the 1990s eroded the preferential access of Palestinian goods in their dominant export market. As a result, imports from the rest of the world have progressively replaced those from the West Bank and Gaza, especially in the main labor-intensive sectors. Partly as a consequence of this shift, manufacturing production in the West Bank and Gaza declined in real terms by almost 20 percent between 1994 and 2009.[37] Palestinian merchandise exports slowed in nominal terms prior to the Second Intifada (figure 1.7), and declined as a share of GDP from over 10 percent in 1996 to less than 9 percent in 1999.[38] Palestinian exports also declined slightly in constant prices during this period. Palestinian exports generally performed worse than Israeli imports.

The limited changes in Palestinian trade as a result of the liberalization of the Israeli import regime mask a large variation across sectors (figure 1.8).[39] For example, exports of cucumbers, and of marble and alabaster, rose by more than $6 million each, while exports of building stone dropped by $8 million. All in all, the shape of the distribution of changes in figure 1.8 suggests that more sectors

Figure 1.7 Palestinian Exports to the World and to Israel, 1996–2000
Thousand US dollars

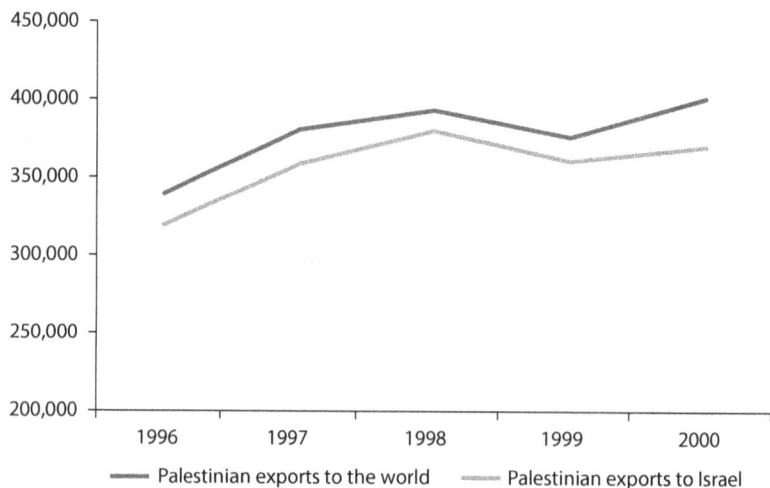

Source: Elaboration on data from the Palestinian Central Bureau of Statistics.

Figure 1.8 Distribution of Changes in Palestinian Exports (1996–99)
Thousand US dollars

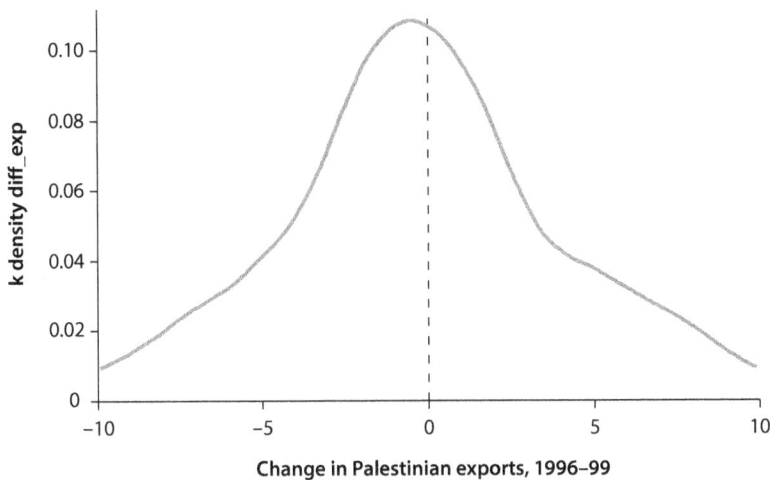

Source: Palestinian Central Bureau of Statistics.
Note: Sectors are recorded at the 5-digit SITC level.

had negative than positive changes, and the large variation in changes likely resulted in very different effects across local areas, depending on where these goods are produced and their degree of labor intensity. This large variation across sectors, and thus across local areas, provides a useful dataset for testing the impact of changes in trade on the Second Intifada.

As in previous studies (Calì and Miaari 2013; Miaari, Zussman, and Zussman 2014), the number of Palestinian fatalities killed by Israeli forces is the main measure of conflict intensity across the West Bank and Gaza. This is a suitable measure as most of these fatalities were the result of political demonstrations suppressed by the Israeli army or direct confrontation between the Israeli army and Palestinian armed factions. The evolution of Palestinian fatalities, depicted in figure 1.9, shows that violence in the West Bank peaked in 2002 and declined through 2003 and 2004, when the Second Intifada finally drew to a close. This period was followed by periods of relatively low-intensity conflict. In Gaza, after the drop in 2003, violence picked up again in 2004 and lasted until the first half of 2005. During the respective sample periods, 1,278 Palestinian fatalities were recorded in the West Bank. In Gaza, 1,702 Palestinian fatalities were recorded.

Empirical Results—Exports

We find that changes in Palestinian exports had a significant impact on conflict intensity during the Second Intifada. We model conflict intensity (the number of conflict-related fatalities in a locality) as a function of changes in overall sectoral exports weighted by the share of that sector in each locality's private employment, along with indicators of sociodemographic conditions, the quality of

Figure 1.9 Palestinians Killed by Israel in the West Bank and Gaza, 2000–04
Number of deaths

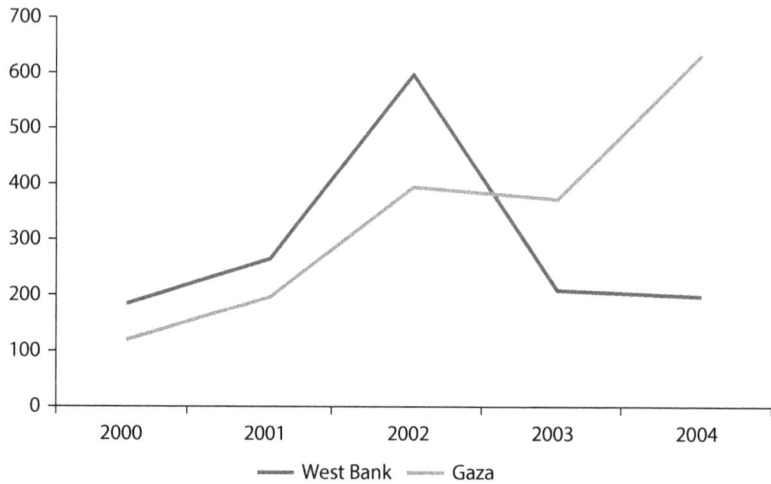

Source: B'tselem.

infrastructure, and the region (West Bank, Jerusalem, or Gaza).[40] An increase of $10 million in the export revenue variable reduces conflict-related fatalities in that locality by 2.1 percent, significant at the 1 percent level (column 1 of table B.15).[41] Given the weighting scheme for the export variable, this effect reflects the conflict-reducing impact of exports via employment. Adding economic controls, including permits to work in Israel and the unemployment rate, as well as the Palestinian fatalities prior to the Second Intifada (1995–2000), slightly raises the absolute size of the export coefficient, which remains significant at 1 percent (column 2 of table B.15).

These results support the opportunity cost hypothesis: better employment opportunities should raise the opportunity cost of involvement in the conflict, thus lowering its intensity. This result is also in line with experts' opinion on the determinants of violence in the West Bank in the current phase (Xinhua 2014).[42]

We next add other labor market indicators from the Palestinian Labor Force Survey (PLFS), including the share of private and public employment in the locality, the share of the locality's workers who are employed in Israel, and the average wage in 1999 (column 3 of table B.15). Adding these potentially important controls, which capture the pre-Intifada reliance of the localities on different sources of employment, increases the estimated impact of changes in export revenues on the conflict. Now a rise in $10 million in Palestinian exports of a sector covering 10 percent of the locality's private employment reduces conflict-related fatalities in that locality by 2.8 percent, significant at the 1 percent level. This larger absolute value of the coefficient is entirely due to the reduction in sample size (to 199 localities) caused by the inclusion of the additional labor market controls.[43] This smaller sample size provides a robustness check in its own right, as it restricts the analysis to comparatively larger localities.

Thus far, we have constrained the effect of exports on conflict to be similar across localities in the West Bank and the Gaza Strip. Testing our preferred specification for the West Bank and the Gaza Strip separately confirms the finding that increases in Palestinian exports are negatively associated with the number of fatalities during the Second Intifada (columns 5 and 6 of table B.15).[44] The results for Gaza should be interpreted with caution since they only rely on a population of 37 localities.

We also estimate the impact on conflict of other control variables used in the export equation. Consistent with the opportunity cost mechanism, a higher level of education and higher private sector wages are associated with lower conflict intensity. Some other control variables have a relatively straightforward interpretation. Higher shares of large households and of married individuals are associated with lower conflict intensity. More permits to work in Israel in 1999 (and higher wages to Palestinian employees in Israel) are associated with a higher number of fatalities during the Second Intifada, probably because Israel imposed employment restrictions at the outset of the Intifada (Miaari, Zussman, and Zussman 2014). More populated localities have a higher number of fatalities, although this association is not robust across specifications.

Empirical Results—Other Trade Variables

Changes in imports are found to have no significant impact on conflict intensity in the next period (column 1 of table B.15). This suggests that the eventual displacement effect of increased imports on domestic producers is not substantial. Alternatively, higher imports may reflect higher demand, and thus better economic conditions. This addition does not affect the coefficient on change in Palestinian exports, which remains significant and of similar magnitude as before.

One possible issue with our results is that Israel might have changed its trade policies in anticipation of the Second Intifada. If so, then our estimate of the impact of exports on conflict would be biased. However, this is unlikely. To show this, we construct a measure of how Israeli imports from the rest of the world may have affected individual Palestinian localities. Similar to our export index, this measure is, for each locality, the weighted average of changes in sectoral imports by Israel from the rest of the world, where the weights are the share of local private employment in that sector. This measurement of the impact of Israeli imports has no significant impact on conflict.[45] This result is consistent with the view that Israel did not change its trade policies in connection to the expected surge in violence during the 1990s. It also suggests that once we control for changes in Palestinian exports, any residual effect of Israeli imports on Palestinian employment is marginal.

A further check on our results involves splitting the export variable into changes in exports to Israel and changes in exports to the rest of the world, again weighted by each locality's employment by sector. While both of these variables have a negative relationship with conflict, only the variable reflecting exports to Israel is statistically significant.[46] It thus appears that exports to Israel were the main channel through which exports affected violence during the Second Intifada, which is not surprising as Israel accounted for over 90 percent of Palestinian exports in the 1990s. However, the large absolute magnitude of the coefficient on exports to the rest of the world suggests potentially relevant effect on conflict from those exports as well.

Empirical Results—Alternative Measures of Conflict

So far we have used the total number of Palestinians killed by Israeli forces as the measure of conflict intensity. However, some of these fatalities were not related to Palestinian participation in politically motivated violence against Israeli forces. The B'tselem dataset does identify various instances of Palestinians who were not taking part in the hostilities, but were killed by Israeli forces. Those fatalities should not be considered when testing for the opportunity cost motive to engage in violence. To address this issue we use as the dependent variable only the number of Palestinian fatalities as a result of participation in violence against Israeli forces or political demonstrations. We do not use this dependent variable for our main specification, because information on participation in violence is not provided for every recorded fatality. The estimate for the impact of exports on conflict remains significant with this alternative dependent variable. In fact, the estimated impact is larger than in our main specification, and (contrary to the results given above) with this dependent variable the coefficient on exports to the rest of the world becomes significant at the 10 percent level (see column 3 of table B.17). The import variables continue to be irrelevant in explaining conflict intensity.

Changes in Palestinian exports also affect the probability of conflict. Here we define a dependent variable equal to 1 if a locality experiences any fatalities throughout the Second Intifada and zero otherwise. The coefficient on the export variable indicates that an increase in Palestinian exports by $10 million in a sector employing 10 percent of private employees in a locality reduces the probability of conflict in that locality by between 5.3 percent and 5.5 percent (columns 1–2 in table B.18).[47] This effect increases to between 6.3 percent and 6.9 percent in the case of exports to Israel, while it is not significant for the exports to the rest of the world (columns 3–4). Again, the effect of changes in imports is not significant (columns 2 and 4).

Empirical Results—The Issue of Endogeneity

One assumption of the econometric techniques used in these estimations is that our trade measures are exogenous, that is, they are not affected by the dependent variable (conflict intensity or probability of conflict), nor are they related to other unobserved factors affecting also local conflict. This assumption appears to be plausible for a number of reasons. First, as the distribution of employment across sectors in each locality is measured at the beginning of the period, it should not be affected by the eruption of the local-level conflict after three years.

Second, controlling for a large number of local-level factors should help address the concern that employment shares may reflect local characteristics such as skill intensity and labor productivity that may also drive conflict locally. Third, given the large number of localities, each of them should not exert an important influence over the export variable, which is the aggregation over all Palestinian localities. Finally, these changes in trade, and exports in particular, are mainly driven by two factors exogenous to the Palestinian economy. The first is the emergence of new global suppliers, chiefly China, competing in similar sectors (and markets) where Palestinian exports are concentrated. The second is the reduction in Israeli import tariffs during the 1990s, which eroded the preferential access of Palestinian exporters to their most important external market.

It is nevertheless useful to check whether our trade values are indeed exogenous. As with the Nigeria case study, we select two alternative variables (called instruments) that are related to our export variable but are demonstrably not influenced by conditions in Palestinian localities. The first instrument is the change in Chinese export supply over the same period as our export variable (1996–99). This is arguably an important source of competition for Palestinian exports, especially in Israel. Indeed, unlike imports from the West Bank and Gaza, Israeli imports from China dramatically increased between 1995 and 2000 (figure 1.10). In order to ensure that our measure of Chinese exports is not affected by conditions in Israel (which might possibly be related to the prospects for conflict), we take the changes in Chinese sectoral exports to the world, excluding Israel. The second instrument is the 1990s decline in Israeli import duties in most sectors, which reduced Palestinian exporters' preferential access to the Israeli market, thus reducing the demand for Palestinian goods.

Figure 1.10 Israeli Imports from China and the West Bank and Gaza, 1995–2000
Million US dollars

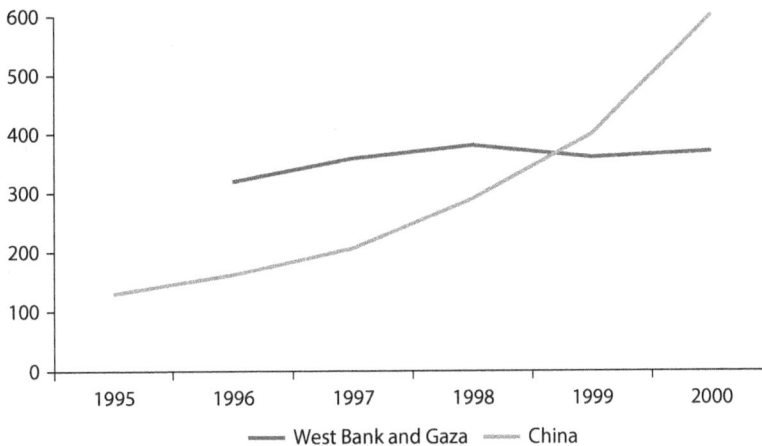

Sources: UN Commodity Trade Statistics Database and Palestinian Central Bureau of Statistics.

Both of these instruments are effective predictors of Palestinian exports. And these predictions of Palestinian exports are significantly related to conflict intensity during the Second Intifada. We can therefore conclude that our export variable is not driven by conditions in the West Bank and Gaza, so that our estimation of the impact of Palestinian exports on conflict intensity is not affected by endogeneity. A more formal description of the procedure used to test for endogeneity is given in appendix B.

Empirical Results—Conclusions

Overall, the results suggest that changes in Palestinian exports (to Israel and to a more limited extent to the rest of the world) during the period before the Second Intifada reduce the intensity (and the probability) of conflict during the Second intifada. An increase of $10 million in Palestinian exports of a sector employing 10 percent of a locality's private employment reduces conflict-related fatalities in that locality by between 2.1 percent and 2.8 percent. This increase also reduces the probability of the eruption of conflict in the locality by between 5.3 percent and 5.5 percent.

Each of the trade variables is the weighted average of changes in exports (or imports) by sector, where the weights reflect the sectoral distribution of private employment in each locality. Therefore, these results can be interpreted as the outcome of variation in employment opportunities induced by export (and import) changes. These findings support the opportunity cost hypothesis, that participation in violence increases with declines in real incomes, since the cost in terms of foregone income declines.

The Israeli-Palestinian conflict provides an unusually straightforward test of the opportunity cost hypothesis. That is, some studies find that export prices are positively related to conflict, because competition for valuable, point-source commodities intensifies as their price rises. This channel is unlikely to operate in the Israeli-Palestinian context, as the Palestinian export basket does not include such goods. Similarly, some studies find a positive relationship between agricultural commodity prices and conflict, because increases in the revenues from agriculture are used to fund rebel activities. This channel is also unlikely to operate in the Palestinian context, because of the relative inability of the Palestinian authority to tax earnings or trade.

Implications for Trade Policies Affecting the West Bank and Gaza

Our findings suggest that dealing with adverse employment shocks is critical to avert conflict, or reduce its intensity, in fragile environments. The promotion of labor-intensive export sectors appears to be a useful strategy in this context. The evidence in the paper suggests that the policies of fragile country's trading partners can effectively encourage exports, for example by increasing preferential market access.

Facilitating Palestinian trade can be an important strategy to reduce the risk of conflict. This entails better control by Palestinians of their own border, an improved system for tax collection, and renewed trade agreements with Israel on a more equal footing. Improving trade will also require the development of a strong Palestinian private sector. A large amount of evidence suggests that this development cannot be achieved without the removal of the many Israeli measures which restrict the activity of the Palestinian private sector, such as movement and access restrictions, the West Bank wall, the blockade in Gaza, and impediments to access to natural resources (Cali and Miaari 2013; UNCTAD 2011; World Bank 2007; Niksic et al. 2014).

In addition, our results point to the crucial importance of Palestinian sales to the Israeli market (rather than to any other market) as a way to reduce the probability of intense conflict. On the one hand, this suggests the importance of facilitating the purchase of Palestinian goods and services by Israelis. That is also in line with the finding by Miaari, Zussman, and Zussman (2014) on Palestinian workers in Israel. On the other hand, this dependence on Israel implies a high exposure of the Palestinian private sector to changes in the Israeli market, such as the Israeli trade liberalization of the 1990s. As we have shown, such economic shocks can have important consequences for conflict. Therefore, Palestinian exporters need to be able to diversify their markets. Intensifying trade links with the Arab economies would be a natural starting point. That would require Palestinian sovereignty over its own trade policy, as well as the development of trade facilitation measures linking the West Bank and Gaza with neighboring Arab countries.

Finally, our findings support the hypothesis that economic opportunities affect the dynamics of the Israeli-Palestinian conflict. How to guarantee such opportunities and how changes in trade policies might interact with local political institutions operating within the Palestinian-Israeli conflict are fruitful avenues for future research.

Notes

1. The measurement of export concentration used is the herfindahl index, where higher values indicate greater concentration.

2. Figures obtained via MIT's *Observatory of Economic Complexity* at atlas.media.mit.edu (see Hausmann et al. 2011; Simoes and Hidalgo 2011).

3. Based on available WDI data for 22 fragile countries from the OECD list. The difference was statistically significant at the 0.05 level.

4. When incomes and employment are higher, so is the expected income foregone due to allocating time to violence rather than to an economically productive activity.

5. This rapacity channel is also supported by an emerging literature which finds that aid may increase violence in conflict contexts by raising the value of contestable resources that groups fight over (Nunn and Qian 2013).

6. This mechanism can plausibly account for some of the "resource curse" hypothesis (van der Ploeg 2011), whereby resource rich countries tend to have worse economic performance than other countries.

7. That stability can also be (and in fact it is often) associated with authoritarian, non-democratic political regimes.

8. This information is based on the report by Kesan (2012) as well as personal communications with the main author of the report.

9. This effect is likely to be smaller the larger is the mobility of labor across industries, which would allow workers to adjust to negative industry-specific shocks.

10. In fact, if the reduction in the incentive to produce is large enough to substantially reduce domestic production, the net effect of an export ban could even be negative for consumers.

11. Carter and Bates (2012) argue that that is the case only in countries where there is little political competition (i.e. authoritarian governments) while democracies have to please the majority of the voters, who reside in rural areas in a typical low-income country.

12. The authors define a "regional war complex" as a conflict which has high foreign participation, and domestic participation inside at least one of the countries involved in the violent conflict that is high enough to challenge the government's monopoly of force in that country.

13. The same principle explains why countries which have had past bilateral wars are more likely to sign trade agreements with each other (Martin, Mayer, and Thoenig 2012).

14. Gleditsch (2007) also notes that countries support conflicts in neighboring countries to a large extent on the basis of their affinity or antipathies to existing regimes. Trade is one indicator of compatibility between states.

15. Other studies have focused on the impact of trade, including with neighbors, on interstate wars (e.g. Martin, Mayer, and Thoenig 2008).

16. This estimate is conditional on the changes in the export price index in the preceding two periods.

17. Our result is also different from the negative coefficient of Bruckner and Ciccone (2010). However, our specification is not comparable to theirs, as we run the regressions for onset and ending separately on split samples as in Bazzi and Blattman (2014). In addition we also use the log of the price level instead of price change.

18. In the model of Dal Bó and Dal Bó (2011) this would lead to a relatively small size of the appropriative conflict sector, i.e., a low probability of conflict.

19. This result appears to contradict those of two other recent studies, Berman and Couttenier (2014) and Chaudion et al. (2012). However, the former considers only large economic downturns in trading partners (i.e. banking crises) and focuses on conflict eruption at the subnational level. The latter uses the indicator of market demand as an instrument for economic growth rather than as an independent regressor, and no lagged structure is used.

20. In order to test this hypothesis, we replace the *share of trade with neighbors* with the same variable interacted with an RTA dummy which takes the value of 1 for each country-pair that had an RTA between them by the year before the observation. In this way the variable becomes the share of trade with neighbors under RTAs in a country's total trade.

21. As showed in table B.1, this variable has a negative and significant association with *any conflict onset* (columns 1–4), while it has no significant association with *major conflict onset* (columns 5–8).

22. In order to make the regressions comparable, we rerun the regression with PRIO data using the same battle deaths threshold of major conflict as in COW (i.e. at least 1,000 battle deaths over the entire course of the conflict).

23. To save clutter, for each price variable in table B.4 we only report the value and significance of the sum of the three coefficients (the contemporaneous and the two lagged variables). Unless otherwise stated, we also do not report the coefficients of the other trade variables as they are little affected by the splitting of the price indices (results available upon request).

24. The only exception is the first lag of the export price index, which has a negative and significant effect on a conflict ending. However, this effect is offset by that of the contemporaneous and second lag terms, and the sum of the export price index coefficients is not significant.

25. The result is not significant when using fast moving weights (column 5).

26. A drop in demand from a country's main market for an agricultural commodity typically will not greatly affect export volumes, given the opportunities for switching to other markets.

27. Trade may affect the incentive for the neighbors to intervene in a country's conflict also for other reasons than the opportunity cost channel. For example trade may raise the trust between the peoples of the neighboring countries (Rohner, Thoenig, and Zilibotti 2013) thus reducing the propensity of countries to fuel conflict in their neighbors.

28. The land rights related to indigenous people are of particular concern for Fulani pastoralist in Plateau (and other states), as pastoralists by definition do not own the land their herds graze upon when they are on the move. Expanding cities and agriculture, in addition to the outermost northern pastoralist routes becoming irregularly dry, has led the Fulani pastoralists to clash with farmers, many of whom are indigenous. This is not exclusive to Plateau State, as seen in the 2013 small outbreaks of violence in Benue State (Human Rights Watch 2013).

29. There was tension in the state in October 2013 following bloody clashes between Fulani herdsmen and Yoruba inhabitants at Alapa/Onire in Asa Local Government Area of the state.

30. Tables showing the estimated coefficients for each of the independent variables, under various specifications of the model, are presented in appendix B.

31. The lack of significance of the oil price index after 2009 occurs because we can include only one year after the 2009 agreement, as opposed to two years with the use of the lag.

32. The purpose is to control for potential negative autocorrelation of prices over time periods (Bazzi and Blattman 2014).

33. Note we are unable to run the model with fatalities using indices based on broad matching and on international prices due to lack of convergence.

34. In an interview with IRIN Human Rights Watch researcher Eric Guttschuss noted that "Boko Haram is essentially the fallout of frustration with corruption and the attendant social malaise of poverty and unemployment." Similarly Paul Lubeck, a professor at the University of California, Santa Cruz, who studies the group, argues in an interview that Boko Haram tapped into growing anger among northern Nigerians at their poverty and lack of opportunity (Nossiter and Kirkpatrick 2014).

35. Part of this export in the 1990s was due to Israeli firms using Palestinian firms as subcontractors in a number of sectors, such as textile, garments, and furniture.

36. Since the withdrawal of Israel from Gaza in 2005, the border between Gaza and the Arab Republic of Egypt is no longer controlled by Israel although the blockade of Gaza effectively implies no formal trade between Gaza and Egypt.

37. Authors' calculations based on PCBS' National Accounts.

38. Authors' calculations based on PCBS' trade data and National Accounts.

39. The distribution is obtained through a kernel density function (with 1.5 bandwidth).

40. The sociodemographic variables refer to 1997 and include the total population, share of males in the population, share of the population aged 15–40, share of population with elementary education or below, share of households with more than 8 members, and the share of married individuals. We also control for factors that may foster Palestinian grievances, including the availability of public utilities such as water, electricity, sewage, and landline telephones; the unemployment rate in 1997 (computed from the Census); and the number of permits to work in Israel in 1999, which Miaari, Zussman, and Zussman (2014) show to be associated with the subsequent violence. Finally, to control for the cyclicality of the conflict, we include the number of Palestinian fatalities in each locality between January 1995 and August 2000.

41. Marginal effects are calculated as incidence rate ratios and are equal to 1-e.

42. The agency reports that Yoram Cohen, the chief of Israel's Shin Bet security agency, in a meeting of the Knesset Foreign and Security Affairs Committee in February 2014 argued that "the uptick in Palestinian militant attacks against Israelis in the past year can be traced back to the economic grievances Palestinians are suffering from in the West Bank" (Xinhua 2014).

43. In fact this inclusion reduces the absolute size of the export coefficient (from –0.159 in column 4 of table B.16 to –0.137 in column 3). Column 4 uses the same specification as in column 2 but run over this restricted sample.

44. The coefficient is more precisely estimated in the West Bank than in Gaza, probably due to the small sample size in the latter. However it is larger in magnitude in Gaza.

45. The period covered is 1996–1999. We subtract Palestinian imports from Israel from the Israeli imports from the rest of the world, as a large part of Palestinian imports are processed through Israeli firms and are recorded as part of Israel's total imports. The result is also robust to including Palestinian imports from Israel (results available from the authors upon request).

46. Although even the exports to Israel variable is significant only at the 15 percent level over the Palestinian Labor Force Survey sample, with import variables included in the estimation (see column 7 of table B.17).

47. This estimation uses a probit model. The impact of exports on the probability of conflict increases to between 6.3 percent and 6.9 percent in the case of exports to Israel, while is it not significant for the exports to the rest of the world (columns 3 and 4 of table B.20). Again, the effect of changes in imports is not significant (columns 2 and 4).

References

ACLED. 2013. *Country Report: Nigeria.* April.

Aksoy, A., and F. Ng. 2008. "Who Are the Net Food Importing Countries?" Policy Research Working Paper 4457, World Bank.

Angrist, J., and A. Kugler. 2008. "Rural Windfall or a New Resource Curse? Coca, Income, and Civil Conflict in Colombia." *The Review of Economics and Statistics* 90 (2): 191–215.

Arezki, R., and M. Brückner. 2011. "Food Prices, Conflict, and Democratic Change." Mimeo.

Bank of Israel. 2010. "Recent Economic Developments." *Tel Aviv*, May–August, 128.

Bazzi, S., and C. Blattman. 2014. "Economic Shocks and Conflict: Evidence from Commodity Prices." *American Economic Journal: Macroeconomics.*

Becker, G. 1968. "Crime and Punishment: An Economic Approach." *Journal of Political Economy* 76: 169–217.

Bellemare, M. F. 2011. "Rising Food Prices, Food Price Volatility, and Political Unrest." Duke University, Mimeo.

Bellows, J., and E. Miguel. 2009. "War and Local Collective Action in Sierra Leone." *Journal of Public Economics* 93 (11–12): 1144–57.

Berman, N., and M. Couttenier. 2014. "External Shocks, Internal Shots: The Geography of Civil Conflicts." CEPR Discussion Paper 9895.

Berrebi, C. 2007. "Evidence about the Link between Education, Poverty and Terrorism among Palestinians." *Peace Economics, Peace Science and Public Policy* 13 (1): Article 2.

Besley, T., and T. Persson. 2008. "The Incidence of Civil War: Theory and Evidence." Mimeo.

Bhavnani, R. R., and S. Jha. 2011. "Trade Shocks, Mass Mobilization and Decolonization: Evidence from India's Independence Struggle." Mimeo.

Blattman, C., and E. Miguel. 2010. "Civil War." *Journal of Economic Literature* 48: 3–57.

Bruckner, M., and A. Ciccone. 2010. "International Commodity Prices, Growth and the Outbreak of Civil War in Sub-Saharan Africa." *The Economic Journal* 120 (May): 519–34.

Buhaug, H., and K. S. Gleditsch. 2008. "Contagion or Confusion? Why Conflicts Cluster in Space." *International Studies Quarterly* 52 (2): 215–33.

Buhaug, H., and J. K. Rod. 2006. "Local Determinants of African Civil Wars, 1970–2001." *Political Geography* 25: 315–35.

Cadot, O., and J. Gourdon. 2012. "Assessing the Price-Raising Effect of Non-Tariff Measures in Africa." CEPII Working Paper 2012–16.

Cali, M., and S. Miaari. 2013. "The Labor Market Impact of Mobility Restrictions: Evidence from the West Bank." Policy Research Working Paper 6457, World Bank.

Cali, M., S. Miaari, and B. Fallah. 2014. "More Jobs, Less Fighting? Evidence from the Second Intifada." Mimeo.

Chaudion, S., Z. Peskowitz, and C. Stanton. 2012. "Beyond Zeroes and Ones: The Effect of Income on the Severity and Evolution of Civil Conflict." Mimeo.

Collier, P., and A. Hoffler. 1998. "On Economic Causes of Civil War." *Oxford Economic Papers* 50 (4): 563–73.

Collier, P., and A. Hoffler. 2004. "Greed and Grievance in Civil War." *Oxford Economic Papers* 56 (4): 563–96.

Copeland, F. 2013. "The Boko Haram Insurgency in Nigeria, Comprehensive Information on Complex Issues." https://www.cimicweb.org/cmo/medbasin/Holder/Documents/r028%20CFC%20Monthly%20Thematic%20Report%20(21-FEB-13).pdf.

Cotet, A. M., and K. K. Tsui. 2013. "Oil and Conflict: What Does the Cross Country Evidence Really Show?" *American Economic Journal: Macroeconomics* 5 (1): 49–80.

Council on Foreign Relations. 2014. "Boko Haram." Background Paper.

Dal Bó, E., and P. Dal Bó. 2011. "Workers, Warriors and Criminals: Social Conflict in General Equilibrium." *Journal of the European Economic Association* 9 (4).

Dube, O., and J. Vargas. 2013. "Commodity Price Shocks and Civil Conflict: Evidence from Colombia." *Review of Economic Studies* 80 (4): 1384–1421.

FAO (Food and Agriculture Organization of the United Nations). 2002. "FAO Papers on Selected Issues Relating to the WTO Negotiations on Agriculture." Commodities and Trade Division, Rome. ftp://ftp.fao.org/docrep/fao/004/Y3733E/Y3733E00.pdf.

Fearon, J., and D. Laitin. 2003. "Ethnicity, Insurgency, and Civil War." *American Political Science Review* 97 (1): 75–90.

Gersovitz, M., and N. Kriger. 2013. "What Is a Civil War? A Critical Review of Its Definition and (Econometric) Consequences." *World Bank Research Observer* 28 (2): 159–90.

Gleditsch, K. S. 2007. "Transnational Dimensions of Civil War." *Journal of Peace Research* 44: 293–309.

Gleditsch, N. P., P. Wallensteen, M. Eriksson, M. Sollenberg, and H. Strand. 2002. "Armed Conflict 1946–2001: A New Dataset." *Journal of Peace Research* 39 (5): 615–37.

Harari, M., and E. La Ferrara. 2012. "Conflict, Climate and Cells: A Disaggregated Analysis." IGIER Working Paper 461, Bocconi University.

Hsiang, S. M., and M. Burke. 2014. "Climate, Conflict, and Social Stability: What Does the Evidence Say?" *Climatic Change* 123: 39–55.

Hull, P., and M. Imai. 2013. "Economic Shocks and Civil Conflict: Evidence from Foreign Interest Rate Movements." *Journal of Development Economics* 103: 77–89.

Independent Evaluation Group. 2011. "Timor-Leste Country Program Evaluation, 2000–2010." Independent Evaluation Group, World Bank, Washington, DC.

International Crisis Group. 2014. *Curbing Violence in Nigeria (II): The Boko Haram Insurgency*, Africa Report 216.

IRIN. 2011a. "Understanding Nigeria's Boko Haram Radicals." July.

———. 2011b. "Analysis: Niger Delta Still Unstable despite Amnesty." November.

Ivanic, M., and W. Martin. 2008. "Implications of Higher Global Food Prices for Poverty in Low-Income Countries." *Agricultural Economics* 39 supplement: 405–16.

Jacoby, H. 2013. "Food Prices, Wages, and Welfare in Rural India." Policy Research Working Paper 6412, World Bank.

Kelleher, S., and J. D. Reyes. 2014. "Technical Measures to Trade in Central America: Incidence, Price Effect, and Consumer Welfare." World Bank Working Paper 6857.

Kesan. 2012. "Economic Development and Peace in Karen State: Scenarios, Principles & Policies." Unpublished report.

King, G., and L. Zeng. 2001. "Logistic Regression in Rare Events Data." *Political Analysis* 9: 137–63.

Lin, Y-H., and G. Michaels. 2011. "Do Giant Oilfield Discoveries Fuel Internal Armed Conflicts?" CEPR Discussion Paper 8620.

Lipton, M. 1977. *Why Poor People Stay Poor: Urban Bias in World Development*. Cambridge, MA: Harvard University Press.

Martin, P., T. Mayer, and M. Thoenig. 2012. "The Geography of Conflicts and Regional Trade Agreements." *AEJ: Macroeconomics* 4 (4): 1–35.

Maystadt, J-F., G. De Luca, P. G. Sekeris, J. Ulimwengu, and R. Folledo. 2014. "Mineral Resources and Conflicts in DRC: A Case of Ecological Fallacy?" *Oxford Economic Papers* 66 (3): 721–49. http://oep.oxfordjournals.org/content/66/3/721.

Maystadt, J.-F., and O. Ecker. 2014 "Extreme Weather and Civil War: Does Drought Fuel Conflict in Somalia through Livestock Price Shocks?" *American Journal of Agricultural Economics.*

Maystadt, J.-F., J.-F. Trinh Tan, and C. Breisinger. 2014. "Does Food Security Matter for Transition in Arab Countries?" *Food Policy* 46: 106–15.

Miaari, S., A. Zussman, and N. Zussman. 2014. "Employment Restrictions and Political Violence in the Israeli-Palestinian Conflict." *Journal of Economic Behavior and Organization* 101 (May): 24–44.

Miguel, E., S. Satyanath, and E. Sergenti. 2004. "Economic Shocks and Civil Conflict: An Instrumental Variables Approach." *Journal of Political Economy* 112 (4): 725–53.

Niksic, O., N. Nasser Eddin, and M. Cali. 2014. *Area C and the Future of the Palestinian Economy.* Washington, DC: World Bank.

Nossiter, A., and D. D. Kirkpatrick. 2014. "Abduction of Girls an Act Not Even Al Qaeda Can Condone." *The New York Times*, May 7.

Nunn, N., and N. Qian. 2014. "U.S. Food Aid and Civil Conflict." *American Economic Review* 104 (6): 1630–66.

OECD. 2013. *Fragile States 2013: Resource Flows and Trends in a Shifting World.* Paris: OECD.

Portugal-Perez, A., and J. S. Wilson. 2012. "Export Performance and Trade Facilitation Reform: Hard and Soft Infrastructure." *World Development* 40 (7): 1295–307.

Revenue Watch Institute. 2013. "The 2013 Resource Governance Index." Washington, DC: Revenue Watch Institute.

Rohner, D., M. Thoenig, and F. Zilibotti. 2013. "War Signals: A Theory of Trade, Trust and Conflict." *Review of Economic Studies* 80 (3): 1114–47.

Saleh, B. A. 2009. "An Econometric Analysis of Palestinian Attacks: An Examination of Deprivation Theory and Choice of Attacks." *European Journal of Social Sciences* 7 (4): 17–29.

Savun, B., and D. C. Tirone. 2012. "Exogenous Shocks, Foreign Aid, and Civil War." *International Organization* 66: 363–93.

Sayne, A. 2013. *What's Next for Security in the Niger Delta?* U.S. Institute for Peace Special Report 333.

Sayre, E. A. 2009. "Labor Market Conditions, Political Events, and Palestinian Suicide Bombings." *Peace Economics, Peace Science and Public Policy* 15 (1): 1–26.

Simoes, A. J. G., and C. A. Hidalgo. 2011. "The Economic Complexity Observatory: An Analytical Tool for Understanding the Dynamics of Economic Development." Workshops at the Twenty-Fifth AAAI Conference on Artificial Intelligence.

Treichel, V., M. Hoppe, O. Cadot, and J. Gourdon. 2012. "Import Bans in Nigeria Increase Poverty." Africa Trade Policy Note 28, World Bank.

UNCTAD. 2011. *Developments in the Economy of the Occupied Palestinian Territory.* Geneva: UNCTAD Secretariat.

van der Ploeg, F. 2011. "Natural Resources: Curse or Blessing?" *Journal of Economic Literature* 49 (2): 366–420.

World Bank. 2007. *Movement and Access Restrictions in the West Bank: Uncertainty and Inefficiency in the Palestinian Economy.* Washington, DC: World Bank.

———. 2010. "Doing Business Indicators, Trading across Borders." Online data, http://www.doingbusiness.org/data/exploretopics/trading-across-borders.

————. 2011. *World Development Report 2011: Conflict, Security and Development*, Washington, DC: World Bank.

————. 2014a. "Doing Business Indicators, Trading across Borders." Online data. http://www.doingbusiness.org/data/exploretopics/trading-across-borders.

————. 2014b. "World Development Indicators." Online data. http://databank.worldbank.org/data/views/variableSelection/selectvariables.aspx?source=world-development-indicators.

————. 2014c. "Logistics Performance Index." Online data. http://lpi.worldbank.org/.

World Economic Forum. 2014. "Quality of Port Infrastructure." Online data. http://data.worldbank.org/indicator/IQ.WEF.PORT.XQ.

Wudu, W.S. 2013. "Machar Accuses Government of Embezzling $ 4.5 Billion." December 7. http://www.gurtong.net/ECM/Editorial/tabid/124/ctl/ArticleView/mid/519/articleId/14062/Machar-Accuses-Government-Of-Embezzling-45-Billion.aspx.

Xinhua. 2014. "Palestinian Militancy Stems from Economic Hardship: Israeli Security Chief." February 2.

CHAPTER 2

Conditions That Affect the Impact of Trade Shocks on Conflict

Introduction

Changes in economic activity, including those originating in external trade, do not affect peace and stability in a vacuum. Deep-seated factors, often dating back in history, need to be in place in order to create the conditions for conflict and political instability. Norway, Canada, the Republic of South Sudan, and Nigeria are all oil rich economies, but swings in oil prices have little potential to create instability in the first two countries and a great deal of potential in the last two. Changes that affect trade in goods have different effects across countries even in the same region. Increased diamond production and trade, for example, has been associated with higher levels of conflict in the Central African Republic (International Crisis Group 2010) and in Sierra Leone (Bellows and Miguel 2009), but not in Botswana, where the rents from diamonds were shared across all groups in the society. The widespread perception that this sharing agreement was fair helped ensure stability (Robinson, Acemoglu, and Johnson 2003).

These examples point to a basic but often forgotten principle: the expected effects of changes in trade on instability are likely to differ across countries, and across regions within countries. Various factors are likely to facilitate or hinder the extent to which these changes can create instability. Improving our understanding of how the relationship between conflict and changes in trade differs across contexts is important for at least three reasons. First, it would help identify some of the conditions under which changes in trade are more harmful. This information would be important in developing proper monitoring frameworks for future sharp changes in trade volumes or prices. Second, it would allow policy makers to identify, and possibly address, the conditions that make countries vulnerable to changes in trade flows. And third, it would improve our analysis of the extent to which trade-related changes affect conflict. That is, analysis which bundles together countries with very different conditions may conclude that trade-related changes have no impact on conflict, while actually they may be important for conflict, but only in countries that meet certain conditions.

Unfortunately, our understanding of the conditions under which changes in trade trigger conflict remains limited. Scholars have acknowledged the importance of this heterogeneity. Blattman and Miguel (2010, p. 31) note that "there is good reason to believe that the relationships between civil conflict and income shocks … should be conditional ones, evident primarily when interacted with other contextual variables." However, macroeconomic studies of the relationship between trade-related changes and conflict have rarely tested systematically for these condition-ing factors, and no consensus has emerged on their effects.

The local conditions that might affect the relationship between changes in trade and conflict include: (a) grievances that foster tensions among groups, for example generated by economic inequality, ethnic and religious differences, and past conflict events; (b) the state's institutional capacity and political structure, particularly whether government policies foster inclusiveness; (c) conditions in neighboring countries that might encourage or discourage conflict; and (d) policies that affect the transmission of changes in international commodity prices to the domestic market.

In general, our cross-country analysis confirms the expectation that local con-ditions, such as more peaceful neighborhoods, more limited ethnic divisions, lower inequality, and better governance, tend to reduce the impact of changes in trade on conflict. Variables related to grievances and to conditions in neighboring countries appear to be particularly important in this context. While the quality of governance (for example the degree of accountability, level of corruption, and quality of the bureaucracy) has a significant impact on the relationship between export price changes and conflict, the impact of political arrangements (for example the degree of democracy) is more limited. Finally, interventions that slow the transmission of changes in international commodity prices to domestic markets appear to reduce the risk of conflict from changes in export prices, except in the case of point-source commodities.

Similar, although not identical, results emerge from the country case studies. In Nigeria, political factors play an important role in mediating conflict, as the impact of commodity price increases in conflict rises in election years. Delays in the transmission of international prices to local markets reduce the impact of price changes in conflict. Ethnic divisions and economic inequality, but not unem-ployment or poverty rates, magnify the impact of higher oil prices on conflict. Interestingly, past incidents of violence are not shown to increase the impact of commodity prices on conflict. In the West Bank and Gaza, the impact of changes in exports on conflict is increased by the existence of grievances such as the pres-ence of refugees and high unemployment rates, but not the incidence of violent fatalities in the past. Export changes have a greater impact on conflict in localities with a larger share of males (perhaps reflecting a higher share of local residents in Israeli jails), but not in localities with lower levels of education (despite the likeli-hood that more educated individuals face a higher opportunity cost of conflict).

The chapter begins with a brief review of the possible factors mediating the impact of trade-related changes on conflict. The evidence on the interaction between these factors and trade changes in determining conflict is relatively thin, and much of the economic literature on the causes of conflict has focused on changes in income from sources other than external trade. The section titled "Grievances" discusses various kinds of grievances that may affect the relationship between changes in trade and conflict. The section titled "Institutional Capacity and Inclusiveness" does the same for the institutional and political context. The section titled "Conditions in Neighboring Countries" discusses the role of conditions in neighboring countries, and the section titled "Transmission of Prices to Domestic Markets" the transmission of changes in international prices to the domestic market. We then test some of the tentative hypotheses based on this review. The section titled "Cross-Country Empirical Tests" expands on the models discussed in chapter 1 to provide an empirical test of the importance of these factors across countries. The next two sections do the same for our two case studies, Nigeria and the West Bank and Gaza.

Grievances

The literature suggests—albeit with some relevant exceptions—that grievances are a major source of conflict and political unrest. Grievances may arise from a variety of factors, such as the exclusion of certain groups from access to resources and/or political participation, inequality in ownership of assets and in opportunities, or past injustices that have not been redressed. All of these factors can be direct determinants of conflict, but can also create conditions that result in trade-related changes having an impact on conflict. In order to illustrate the relationship between grievances and the impact of trade on conflict, we focus on three important determinants of grievances: ethnic divisions, economic inequality, and past incidence of violence. Unfortunately, the evidence on the importance of these factors in determining the outcome of trade-related changes on conflict is extremely limited. Instead, we rely on evidence on the interaction between general changes in real incomes and grievances in determining conflict.

Ethnic/Religious Differences
Divisions along ethnic lines have been associated with adverse economic and political outcomes. Easterly and Levine (1997) and Alesina et al. (2003) argue that African countries that are more divided along ethnic and linguistic lines are more susceptible to competitive rent-seeking across different groups. One consequence is that these countries are less likely to develop the public goods of infrastructure, education, and strong political institutions necessary to sustain economic growth. Another consequence of these kinds of division is a greater tendency toward conflict (Buhaug, Cederman, and Gleditsch 2011; Cederman, Girardin, and Gleditsch 2009), although this finding is controversial (Collier and Hoeffler 2004; Fearon and Laitin 2003). More recent evidence supports the idea that ethnic and religious diversity plays a key role in conflict across communities within a country. For example, Blair, Blattman, and Hartman (2012) find that ethnic and religious diversity is one the most powerful predictors of the onset of conflict in 247 communities in Liberia. The risk of conflict appears to be lower in communities populated predominately or exclusively by a single tribe.

Other studies provide evidence that the role of ethnic divisions is important in understanding the impact of changes in income on civil conflict (Hull and Imai 2013) and political risk (Bruekner and Gradstein 2014).[1]

The direct effect of ethnic divisions on conflict suggests that political stability may be more vulnerable to economic changes in ethnically polarized countries than in more ethnically homogenous countries. Blimes (2006) finds that ethnic cleavages have an important role in conditioning the effects of various determinants of conflict. In his cross-country analysis, he finds that these effects are underestimated for countries with higher levels of ethnic cleavages and overestimated for those with lower levels. Bruekner and Gradstein (2014) also find that the higher the degree of a country's ethnic polarization, the more adverse is the impact of income growth on political risk.[2] By contrast, Hull and Imai (2013) find that the higher the degree of ethnic fractionalization, the more that income growth reduces conflict (and the more that recessions increase conflict).[3] The diverging results found in Bruekner and Gradstein (2014), who measure polarization, and Hull and Imai (2013), who measure fractionalization, are consistent with other studies suggesting that these two concepts may have opposite effects on conflict (Montalvo and Reynal-Querol 2005). Alternatively, these different results may reflect methodological differences between the two studies, such as the dependent variables used and the source of the change in real incomes.[4] In any event, this difference in the empirical findings is striking and calls for investigation into how ethnic diversity affects the relationship between trade-related changes and conflict.

Economic Inequality

Grievances may be generated by economic inequality. However, the extent to which this type of grievance generates conflict is disputed. Collier and Hoeffler (2004) and Fearon and Laitin (2003) find no support for this hypothesis across countries. Acemoglu and Robinson (2006) note that with high asset inequality, the wealthy may be more willing to invest in repression in order to deter revolution. However, income inequality has been found to increase conflict where conflicts have a strong component of political ideology. For example, income and asset inequality have been shown to be key determinants of Nepal's Maoist insurgency (Nepal, Bohara, and Gawande 2011), the Maoist/Naxalite conflict in India (Gomes 2011), and the conflict in South Mexico (Maystadt 2008).

Inequality in land ownership is particularly important in developing countries, because land often represents a major household asset, offers key income opportunities, and serves as the main collateral for rural dwellers' access to credit. Inequality in land ownership often is manifested in a high percentage of landless households. In this case, a reduction in real incomes may increase the incentive of the population to rebel. For example, Hidalgo et al. (2010) find that reductions in real incomes induced by adverse weather caused the rural poor to invade large landholdings, and that this effect was twice as large in municipalities with high land inequality than in municipalities with low land inequality. Hidalgo et al. (2010) is one of the rare empirical studies on the mediating power of inequality in the relation between economic shocks and conflict.

Incidence of Past Conflict

One of the reasons why countries tend to fall back into conflict is that their citizens carry the burden of past violence and injustice. This burden may increase the sensitivity of these countries to changes in economic conditions. Blair, Blattman, and Hartman (2012) identify the presence of ex-combatants and the exposure to wartime violence as one of the four factors predicting intra-communal violence in Liberia. This finding is consistent with the idea that the experiences of wartime violence may continue to foment tensions even in peacetime. Past victimization, participation in war, and loss of land during the war are all associated with the future likelihood of violence in Liberia (Blair, Blattman, and Hartman 2012). Evidence from the Israeli-Palestinian conflict also supports the notion that past violence is related to successive violence (Miaari, Zussman, and Zussman 2014). However, we are not aware of any studies that relate the sensitivity of trade-related changes to grievances from past violence.

Institutional Capacity and Inclusiveness

The effectiveness of government institutions, and the degree to which government strives to take the concerns of minorities in consideration when formulating policies, are likely to be important in determining whether trade-related changes have a significant impact on the onset or intensity of conflict.

Institutional Capacity

One of the mechanisms through which changes in trade may affect conflict is by raising the value of the "prize" of the conflict. However, the extent to which such a "prize" can be appropriated through fighting also depends on the capacity of the state to maintain control over the resources. The higher such capacity, the higher the probability that increases in the value of disputable wealth may be appropriated by the state, e.g. through higher fiscal revenues, rather than used by insurgents. For example, Angrist and Kugler (2008) argue that the weakness of the Colombian government in the countryside allowed guerrillas and paramilitaries to raise revenues from increased coca prices at the end of the 1990s. That helps explain why the rural areas which expanded coca production subsequently became considerably more violent, while urban areas were virtually unaffected.

The issue of state capacity may be particularly important for oil exporters. Fearon (2005) argues that these countries are particularly prone to civil war because of their relatively weak state institutions, at least compared to other countries with similar per capita income levels. States with high oil revenues tend to have less incentive to develop administrative capabilities and control of their territory (Fearon and Laitin 2003). This relatively low state capacity may also make oil wealth a particularly attractive prize for potential insurgents.

Type of Political Regime

While it seems reasonable that states with more effective institutions are better at mitigating the potential impact of trade change on conflict, it is more difficult to evaluate whether more inclusive governments, or alternatively more democratic governments, are more effective in this context. One view is that countries with more inclusive state institutions, or stronger democratic institutions (Miguel, Satyanath, and Sergenti 2004), may be better able to negotiate compromises among social groups to avoid unrest in the face of an adverse change in trade. On the other hand, strong, authoritarian states that are not viewed as inclusive may use increases in the prices of their exports (or reductions in the prices of their imports) to ramp up military repression, rather than expanding social expenditures to pacify the population. It will be difficult to distinguish in empirical analysis between a reduction in conflict owing to greater repression versus a reduction owing to a more inclusive approach to government, as in either case the probability of conflict onset (or its intensity) would decrease.

The empirical evidence is mixed. Besley and Persson (2008) find that commodity prices affect conflict only in countries with weak constraints on executive power. Their empirical results confirm diametrically different effects of commodity price changes between parliamentary and nonparliamentary democracies.[5] It is possible that ethnic groups are more likely to have legitimate, effective channels to seek redress of their grievances when checks and balances are strong, than when there is little constraint on executive power. However, this result may just reflect other structural differences between countries with strong constraints, mostly high-income Western democracies, and countries with weak constraints, mostly developing countries. Caselli and Tesei (2013) find that positive commodity price shocks have no effect on political stability when they occur in democracies.

On the other hand, Bazzi and Blattman (2014) find that commodity price changes have no significant impact on conflict when considering only high-risk countries, defined by the type of political system (and, for that matter, the level of economic inequality and the degree of ethnic polarization).[6] Similarly, Miguel, Satyanath, and Sergenti (2004) do not find any difference in the impact of weather shocks on civil war between countries differing in terms of democratic rule, ethno-linguistic fractionalization, type of terrain, income per capita, or oil-exporting status.

How could studies using similar data, variables, and approaches find such different results? Note that the findings of Bazzi and Blattman (2014) and Miguel, Satyanath, and Sergenti (2004) also contradict some of the studies cited above, for example Hull and Imai (2013) and Brueckner and Gradstein (2014) on the importance of ethnic divisions on conflict. One reason is that the studies differ in significant details. The analysis in Miguel, Satyanath, and Sergenti (2004) is not strictly comparable with the others, as they restrict the sample to sub-Saharan African countries. Importantly, Besley and Persson (2008) and Hull and Imai (2013) use a different way of coding civil wars than Bazzi and Blattman (2014) (the latter's approach is explained in appendix A) and Brueckner and Gradstein (2014) examine the impact on political stability rather than on conflict per se. In addition, Bazzi and Blattman (2014) use various conflict datasets and find a significant effect of the conditioning factors in some specifications, although it is not clear in which ones as they do not report the individual interaction terms.

Conditions in Neighboring Countries

External actors—and neighboring countries in particular—can play a key role in triggering and developing a domestic civil conflict. Therefore, a country's political stability is likely affected by the characteristics of countries in the region. Countries in regions with more democracies are less subject to the risk of conflict, and the presence of a conflict in a neighboring country increases the risk of a civil war by almost two-thirds. Gleditsch (2007) finds that the effects of "bad neighborhoods" can be as important, if not more, in determining the risk of conflict than the profile of individual states themselves. In particular, the presence of transboundary ethnic groups increases a country's risk of conflict, particularly if these ties are to groups in a neighboring conflict (Buhaug and Gleditsch 2008). These results—which are consistent with a broad strand of literature emphasizing the ethnically driven motives of third party intervention (alluded to above)—suggest that transnational ethnic linkages constitute a central mechanism for transmitting conflict between countries.

More importantly for our immediate purpose, ties to neighboring countries may also change the likelihood that a trade-related change may trigger a conflict. A conflict in a neighboring country may make it easier for potential rebels to access weapons to stage a rebellion in their own country, taking advantage of political disaffection due to an adverse change in trade. Alternatively, countries that are surrounded by democracies without conflicts and without transnational ethnic links may be less sensitive to the effects of trade changes on conflict.

Transmission of Prices to Domestic Markets

The extent to which changes in international prices affect civil conflict also depends on the transmission of prices from international to domestic markets. In many countries, food price subsidies provide domestic commodity markets some insulation from changes in international prices. For example, the pass-through from international to domestic food prices in the Middle East and North Africa region varies substantially across countries, reflecting different use of consumption subsidies, although some pass through occurs in all of the countries examined (Ianchovichina, Loening, and Wood 2012). The degree of price transmission may also vary by commodity market, as Minot (2011) shows in his analysis of food prices across African countries in 2007–08.

Trade policies, such as price regulation and export bans, can dampen the effects of changes in international prices on the domestic prices of exported commodities. For example, until 1999 the largest exports in Côte d'Ivoire—coffee and cocoa—were regulated by a state-owned marketing board (the Caisse de stabilisation), which fixed producer prices at a guaranteed level. After it was dismantled, changes in international prices were fully transmitted to exporters. Losch (2002) argues that the fall in international cocoa prices in the subsequent years was one of the causes of the ensuing civil and political unrest in the country.[7] Domestic policies that influence commodity price transmission are often motivated by the need to maintain political order. Carter and Bates (2012) find that political competition matters in determining the government's response to agricultural price shocks. In particular, authoritarian governments tend to enact policies that insulate consumers from price hikes, while more democratic ones tend to focus on protecting rural producers. Their findings confirm that failure to account for policies that affect the transmission of international prices to domestic markets can bias analysis of the effects of commodity price shocks on conflict. Similar attention to policies that affect the transmission of prices should be made in analysis within countries, as the extent of price transmission can vary across regions. Berman and Couttenier (2014) find that commodity price shocks have much weaker effects on civil conflict in locations distant from the main seaports through which imports and exports must transit.

Cross-Country Empirical Tests

These four groups of factors are used to estimate the extent to which differences among countries affect the impact of trade on conflict: (a) factors affecting grievances, including income inequality, ethno-linguistic and religious fractionalization and polarization, and the incidence of past conflicts; (b) institutional capacity and inclusiveness, including the type of political system (e.g. parliamentary versus nonparliamentary democracies; federal versus unitary government), proxies for the quality of governance (e.g. bureaucratic quality and degree of government accountability) and proxies for the quality of parties in office (age of party in office and the extent to which parties take an ideological approach to economic issues); (c) conditions in neighboring countries that may affect their general propensity to destabilize their neighbor, including the presence of a conflict in neighboring countries and the country's trade ties with its neighbors; and (d) policies that affect the transmission of international prices to the domestic economy, as measured by the nominal rate of assistance to agricultural markets (Anderson et al. 2008). The full list of conditioning factors is reported in table A.3.

We use the model developed in chapter 1 to evaluate how these conditioning factors affect the impact of trade-related changes on conflict across countries. We multiply each of three trade variables (export price index, import price index, and changes in a country's principal trade markets) by each of the conditioning variables (the result is referred to as an interaction term), using our preferred specification for the relationship between trade changes and conflict (see column 2 of table B.1).[8] Running these regressions separately maximizes the number of observations, as most of the conditioning variables are not available for the entirety of our baseline sample. This strategy also has the advantage of maximizing the degrees of freedom, compared to including all the conditioning variables in one regression.

With 25 conditioning variables and three types of trade variables, we run a total of 75 regressions. We also add a set of regressions using the price index for point-source commodities alone, as this is the main driver of the relationship between the export price index and conflict. To keep the number of coefficients to interpret manageable, we only include the contemporaneous trade variable (and its interaction with the relevant conditioning variable) in the regression, without its lagged terms. We do this for two reasons. First, the coefficient of the contemporaneous variable incorporates to some extent the coefficients of the lagged trade variables, especially for the export price index.[9] Second, the contemporaneous term is of particular interest in and of itself, as in our analysis (and in others) it tends to be the most important one to explain the impact of trade changes on conflict.

We also include dummy variables to control for conditions in countries that do not vary over time. This specification effectively restricts our analysis to those countries where a conflict has begun during our period of analysis (since 1960).

Results

As expected, the impact on conflict of the export price index, and of the export price index for point-source commodities, depends significantly on many of the conditioning variables. Changes in export prices have lower effects on conflict in countries that are located in peaceful neighborhoods, that have lower ethnic divisions and economic inequality, that have better governance, and that have policies that reduce the transmission of international prices to domestic markets.

Variables related to grievances and to conditions in neighboring countries appear to be important in determining the effect of export prices on conflict. Changes in the overall export price index, and the point-source export price index, have no significant effect on the probability of conflict in countries with sufficiently low levels of economic inequality and of ethnic divisions (whether measured through ethnic polarization or fractionalization), in countries that didn't experience any conflict in the previous 10 years, and in countries whose neighbors are not in conflict, or have sufficiently intense trade with their neighbors.

The quality of state institutions, as measured by various dimensions of governance, has a significant impact on the relationship between changes in the export price index and conflict. In particular, changes in export prices have no effect on conflict in countries with a high degree of government accountability, a low degree of corruption, and high bureaucratic quality, although the latter two results do not carry over to prices on point-source commodities. Other potentially relevant measures of governance, such as the rule of law and the presence of the military in the government, do not seem to be important in this context.

Having a federal government appears to consistently reduce the probability that a change in export prices triggers conflict. That may be because regions tend to have greater autonomy under federal systems than under unitary government systems, which may reduce the incentive for challenging the central state at the local level.[10] The other political variables, including the share of programmatic parties (those with an ideological orientation with respect to economic policy) in power, the age of the party in office, whether elections were held the previous year, and the degree of democracy (including also parliamentary democracy) do not yield robust results for either export prices or point-source commodities prices. Democratic countries (i.e. a score higher than 5 – out of 10 – in the polity index) are less subject to the conflict-inducing impact of changes in the prices of point-source commodities, a result broadly in line with Besley and Persson (2008).[11] These results suggest that the type of state institutions, at least as defined through commonly available measures, seem to have a limited impact in determining the effects of export prices on conflict.

Finally, our results support the hypothesis that substantial nominal rates of assistance to agricultural commodities (whether positive or negative) reduce the risk of conflict due to changes in export prices. This finding is consistent with the hypothesis that international prices are transmitted more rapidly to domestic prices in countries with low distortions to agricultural markets (Anderson et al. 2008). However, this result does not hold for changes in the prices of point-source commodities. This finding comes with two notes of caution. First, these distortions also cause reductions in welfare relative to more direct policy instruments aimed to achieve similar domestic policy objectives (Bhagwati 1978; Corden 1971). Second, the effect we are capturing is inherently short term, as prices are eventually transmitted to domestic prices in the longer run (Ivanic and Martin 2013).

On the other hand, the impact on conflict of the price of imports and of changes in demand in trade partners do not appear to be affected by the conditioning factors we analyze. These trade variables have generally no significant impact on conflict across the entire range of the conditioning factors' values. This result underscores the weakness of these variables in explaining conflict onset in our model.

Table 2.1 may be helpful in providing a snapshot of these results, although it requires some explanation. The table reports the range of values of each conditioning variable for which the marginal effect of the export price index (and the point-source price index) on the onset of conflict is not significantly different from zero (at the 10 percent level). We report this range only when in the rest of the values' range the marginal effect is significant. If the marginal effect is always or never statistically different from zero across the entire values' range, then we report "No diff." For example, ethnic polarization (the fourth variable in table 2.1) has values that range between zero and one. For all values of less than 0.37, indicating a low degree of ethnic polarization, the variable has no significant effect on the relationship between trade changes and conflict. However, where ethnic polarization is high, it does have a significant impact. This presentation facilitates identifying those conditions that make certain countries particularly vulnerable or resilient to changes in the export price index.

Some further insight into a subset of our results can be seen in figure 2.1, which shows how two different conditioning factors affect the impact of export prices on conflict. The upper panel presents the curve describing the marginal effect of the price index, along with its 90 percent confidence interval, across the range of values of the accountability measure (from the International Country Risk Guide database). The downward slope indicates that the effect of the price index becomes less significant as one moves from low to high accountability observations (i.e. from left to right).[12] Thus, when accountability is low, the estimated impact of the price index on conflict is almost twice as great as in observations with average accountability. The effect becomes not significantly different

Table 2.1 Under What Conditions Are the Marginal Effects of Trade Shocks Not Significant?

	Type	Range	Px	Point source
Grievance				
Economic inequality	Contin.	[22;65]	<26 or >58	<46 or >52
gini_net	Contin.	[15;75]	<32	<48
gini_market	Contin.	[17;80]	<37	<52
Ethnic polarization	Contin.	[0;1]	<0.37	<0.42
Ethnic fractionalization	Contin.	[0;1]	<0.28	<0.30
Religious fractionalization	Contin.	[0;0.7]	No diff.	<0.28
Religious polarization	Contin.	[0;0.96]	No diff.	<0.49
Any conflict in last 10 yrs	Dummy	[0;1]	0	0
Political institutions				
Elections (t-1)	Dummy	[0;1]	No diff.	Elections
Federal Government	Dummy	[0;1]	1	Federal
Polity2	Contin.	[−10;10]	No diff.	>5
Parliamentary democracy	Dummy	[0;1]	No diff.	No diff.
Programmatic party	3 groups	[0;3]	< or > 2nd tercile	No diff.
Age of party in office	3 groups	[1;191]	No diff.	No diff.
Governance				
Law	Contin.	[0;6]	No diff.	No diff.
Military	Contin.	[0;6]	No diff.	No diff.
Accountability	Contin.	[0;6]	>3	>2.2
Corruption	Contin.	[0;6]	>2.5	No diff.
Bureaucratic	Contin.	[0;4]	>1.5	No diff.
Composite index	Contin.	[12;84.7]	No diff.	No diff.
Neighbors				
Neighbors' conflict (any)	Dummy	[0;1]	0	0
Share trade neighbors RTA	Contin.	[0;0.8]	>0.35	>0.08
Share trade neighbors	Contin.	[0;0.9]	No diff.	>0.24
Price transmission				
NRA (output + input)	3 groups	[−0.9;1.4]	< or > 2nd tercile	No diff.
NRA (output)	3 groups	[−0.9;3.5]	< or > 2nd tercile	No diff.

Note: The column range indicates the range of values taken by each variable in our sample; the column type groups the variables into three types, i.e. continuous, dummy (0 or 1), and 3 groups (the variable is split into three mutually exclusive continuous groups of values). The latter category is included for those variables for which the marginal effect of Px on conflict appeared to be non linear. The other columns report the values of the interaction for which the marginal effect of the relevant trade variable becomes not significantly different from zero (at the 10 percent level); "No diff." indicates either that the marginal effect is always or never statistically different from zero across the distribution of the interactions' values. The variables are defined in table A.3.

from zero once the accountability index rises above 3. Similarly, the upward slop-ing curve in the lower panel indicates that the effect of the price index on conflict becomes larger for observations characterized by at least one conflict in contigu-ous countries. In fact, the effect of the price index (while positive) is not signifi-cantly different from zero for countries in years that they have peaceful neighbors. These results can also be used to determine the relative importance of the condi-tioning factors in explaining the resilience to trade-related changes.

Figure 2.1 Marginal Effects of Px Across the Range of Interaction Variables' Values

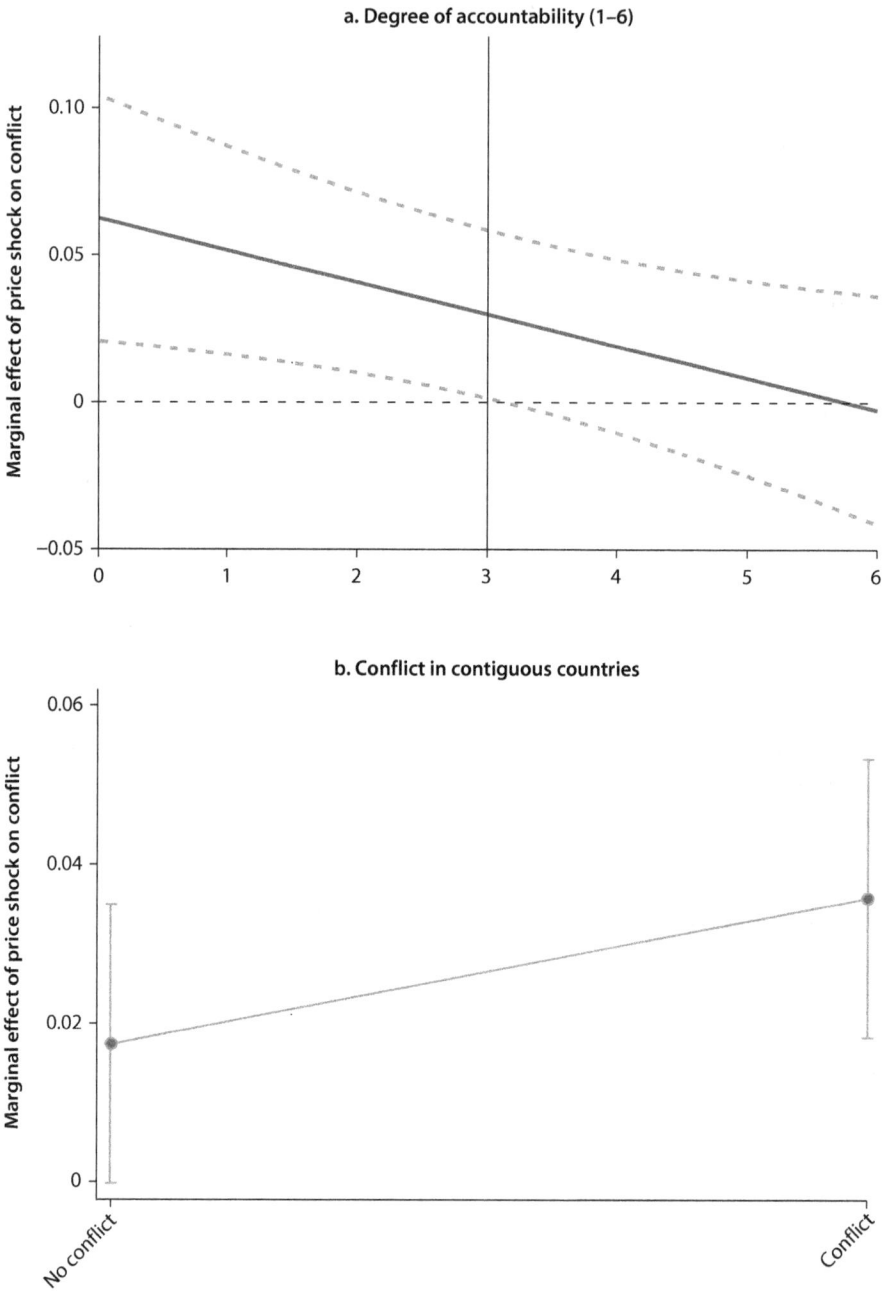

a. Degree of accountability (1–6)

b. Conflict in contiguous countries

Note: The bands indicate the confidence around the estimate line and points represent the 90 percent confidence interval.

The importance of this cross-country heterogeneity is also highlighted by the different association between swings in oil exports and conflict in the Republic of South Sudan and in Timor-Leste, two countries with different degrees of accountability and transparency in oil revenues management (box 1.3 in chapter 1).

These marginal effects of the mediating factors could be used also to predict the risk of conflict from an increase in the value or a new discovery of point-source commodities in a specific country. To illustrate it let us take the example of Lebanon, where recent 3D seismologic mapping of the country's offshore have revealed the likely presence of sizeable hydrocarbon resources. According to some estimates this can be worth several times Lebanon's annual GDP (World Bank 2014). We can apply the estimated coefficients of the interaction terms computed above to the values of the relevant variables for Lebanon to calculate the additional risk of conflict that this discovery would entail.

The country has a relatively high level of economic inequality and of religious fractionalization, and it is experiencing a low-intensity civil conflict.[13] These characteristics increase the risk of conflict induced by hydrocarbons discovery in Lebanon relative to the average country. In table 2.2 we quantify this increased risk due to all the factors that have a statistically significant marginal effect as computed in the regressions underlying table 2.1. On the basis of these marginal effects we know, for example, that for a country with the average level of religious fractionalization (i.e., 0.35), a standard deviation increase in point-source commodity exports raises the risk of conflict by 2.5 percent. At the level of fractionalization of Lebanon (i.e., 0.79) the increased risk is more than double at 5.7 percent. A similar story applies to the two other main factors—economic inequality and the presence of a recent conflict. On the other hand, other factors, such as the level of democracy, the level of accountability, the presence of conflict in neighboring countries, and the share of trade with neighbors, yield smaller differences between Lebanon and the average country.

Table 2.2 Lebanon Has a Higher Risk of Conflict from Hydrocarbons Exports than the Average Country

	Mean	Lebanon	Average effect	LBN effect	Significance
Inequality (Gini)	45.44	55.33	2.1%	4.2%	Yes
Religious fractionalization	0.35	0.79	2.5%	5.7%	Yes
Recent conflict	0.28	1	2.2%	4.1%	Yes
Level of democracy	−1.21	7.00	1.9%	1.9%	No
Accountability	3.24	5.00	2.4%	0.9%	No
Neighbors in conflict	0.52	Yes	2.0%	2.3%	No
Share trade neighbors	0.12	0.03	2.0%	2.1%	No

Source: Computations in the table are based on the following sources for the *Mean* and *Lebanon* values shown: Standardized World Income Inequality Database for inequality data; Alesina et al. (2003) for religious fractionalization; UCDP/PRIO (for mean) and ICRG for Lebanon (see endnote 13 for more details) for recent conflict; polity 2 data for level of democracy; ICRG for accountability; UCDP/Prio (for mean) and ICRG for neighboring conflict; COMTRADE for share of trade with neighbors.
Note: Mean is the mean value of the variable across the entire sample over which the marginal effects of the export price index are computed in the regressions underlying table 2.1; *Lebanon* is the value of the variable for Lebanon (latest available); *Average effect* is the increased probability of conflict due to a standard deviation increase in the point-source commodity export index measured for the mean value of the variable; *LBN effect* is the same increased probability measured at the value of the variable for Lebanon; and *Significance* indicates whether the marginal effect of the variable is significant.

Testing for the Importance of Heterogeneity in the Nigerian Conflict

Chapter 1 found that producer prices, consumer prices, and oil prices appear to be important determinants of conflict across Nigerian states, on average. However, states' vulnerability to a change in a price index may vary. In particular, the presence of deep-seated roots of conflict is usually a necessary condition for any change in real incomes, including that generated by changes in trade prices, to have an impact on violence. A better understanding of what conditions matter in this respect could help direct policy interventions to address the vulnerability to increases in conflict from trade changes.

We consider how political issues, the conditions affecting the transmission of prices, and grievances may affect the impact of changes in trade on conflict across Nigerian states. The procedure is to multiply each factor times the price indices for production, consumption, and (usually) oil. The role of politics is represented by a dummy variable for an election year. As in other African countries (Ksoll, Macchiavello, and Morjaria 2010), elections are perilous times in Nigeria.

The degree of transmission of international prices to the domestic markets is measured by the distance to Lagos for each state. Internal trade costs are high in Nigeria (Atkin and Donaldson 2014). As Lagos is the largest market and the international gateway for the country's trade, distance to Lagos could affect the extent to which changes in international prices translate at the local level. We do not follow this procedure for the oil index, as price transmission should not be an issue for oil.

We use variables representing ethnic divisions, economic inequality, and the level of past conflict intensity to capture the extent to which grievances affect the impact of price changes on conflict. Among the factors affecting grievances, ethnic divisions feature prominently in African conflicts, and in Nigeria in particular (NNoli 2003). Ethnic divisions are represented by the three dummy variables used in chapter 1 as controls: whether the president has the same ethnicity as the dominant group, whether there are more than two significant ethnic minorities, and whether there are multiple dominant ethnic groups in the state.

We use poverty measures, including the poverty gap, the poverty headcount, the gini index of inequality, and the unemployment rate (all computed at the beginning of the period in 2003–04) to reflect the potential for economic conditions contributing to grievances.

Finally, we assume that the level of past conflict will affect the extent to which price indices affect current conflicts. The level of past conflict is an important predictor of future violence by generating grievances (World Bank 2011), a finding that has been confirmed in this analysis as well.

We conduct several repetitions of our preferred specification for the Nigeria model. In each repetition, we add three (only two for the price transmission variable) new terms, which are each of the three price indices multiplied by one of the mediating factors listed above. Further, we repeat this exercise with the different measures of conflict as dependent variables. The results of this analysis are presented in table B.13, which reports only the coefficient of the additions to the separate regressions, along with their degree of significance.

Various findings emerge. First the magnitude of the price effects on conflict is amplified in election years, especially for consumption and oil. Second, the effects of the production price indices on conflict events and on battle events are reduced the farther one moves away from Lagos. Third, various factors related to grievances significantly magnify the conflict-inducing effect of a rise in the price of oil. That is particularly the case for our measurements of ethnic factors and economic inequality.

On the other hand, and more surprisingly, most past conflict events do not magnify the effects of prices on conflict. Past protests are an exception (i.e. the impact of prices on the incidence of protests is higher in states with a past history of protests). In addition, neither unemployment nor poverty appears to affect the impact of prices on conflict.

Heterogeneity in the Israeli-Palestinian Conflict

In chapter 1 we show that changes in exports exert a sizable effect on conflict across Palestinian localities, on average. However, these effects may differ across localities, depending on conditioning factors that could shape the importance of the opportunity cost channel of conflict. The conditions we consider include the share of refugees, the unemployment rate, the share of males, past fatalities, the level of education, and the share of young adult males in the population. As above, we multiply each conditioning factor times the export variable, and include this interaction term in the regression equation, along with the export variable and the controls mentioned in chapter 1.

Changes in exports appear to affect conflict more in localities with a higher share of refugees and a higher unemployment rate, pointing to the importance of grievances in exacerbating the impact of adverse trade changes on conflict.[14] In particular, refugee status is connected with the displacement by Palestinians as a result of the creation of the state of Israel in 1948, which is often associated with Palestinian grievances vis-à-vis Israel. On the other hand, past fatalities, presumably an important indicator of grievances, does not significantly affect the impact of export changes on conflict.[15] A lower share of males (but not of young adult males) in the population is associated with a greater impact of export changes on conflict. A lower share of males in the local population may mean that a higher share of males related to local residents are in Israeli jails, so that this finding also reflects the impact of grievances. Perhaps surprisingly, the level of education is not associated with significantly different effects of changes in exports on conflict intensity.

Notes

1. The former study captures ethnic divisions via the ethno-linguistic fractionalization index, while the latter focuses on ethnic polarization from Montalvo and Reynal-Querol (2005).

2. Ethnic polarization refers to the extent to which most of the population in a country or region is divided between two ethnic or linguistic groups. Ethnic fractionalization refers to the probability that two randomly selected individuals will belong to different ethnic or linguistic groups.

3. These results support the argument by Fearon (2005) that slowed economic development may widen preexisting ethnic rifts in countries with highly fractionalized societies.

4. In particular, Hull and Imai (2013) use a measure of instability (conflict onset) more relevant to the arguments discussed here.

5. This distinction is defined according to Persson and Tabellini (2003).

6. In particular, these subsets of countries include nondemocracies, autocracies, regimes with low executive constraints, low-income countries, highly unequal countries, countries with high ethnic polarization, and countries in sub-Saharan Africa.

7. These price stabilization mechanisms may point toward a second order effect of international price changes on conflict, i.e. via price variability (higher price variability may lead to greater unrest due to the higher variability of incomes). There has been no empirical evidence so far on the extent to which such variability may affect violence.

8. The dependent variable includes all conflicts that result in at least 25 deaths per year. We are mainly interested in modeling the cross-country heterogeneity in the effect of trade-related changes on conflict. Therefore, we do not interact the conditioning variables with the share of trade with neighbors' variables (results for this separate set of regressions are available upon request).

9. Compare the significance of the coefficients in table B.8 vis-à-vis the joint coefficients in table B.1, column 2 and table B.2, column 1.

10. For example, regions within federal countries tend to have more influence over the allocation of natural resource revenues in their territory (Brosio and Singh 2014), which our empirical results suggest is a potentially contentious issue in fragile countries.

11. However, unlike Besley and Persson (2008), these changes in prices do not exert any differential impact on conflict in parliamentary democracies versus other forms of governments.

12. Each observation is one country example for one year.

13. This conflict categorization follows from the International Country Risk Guide (ICGR) data as the UDCP/PRIO armed conflict database. In the first seven months of 2014, ICRG assigns an average value of 2 to Lebanon in the "civil war" category (on a scale of 1 to 4), placing the country in the top decile of that category. The current low-intensity conflict in Lebanon would also be in line with the definition of UCDP/PRIO of "a contested incompatibility that concerns government and/or territory where the use of armed force between two parties, of which at least one is the government of a state, results in at least 25 battle-related deaths."

14. The results are presented in table B.22, where we include one interaction term at a time along with all the usual controls (columns 1–7) and then all of them together (column 8).

15. Note that chapter 1 shows that past violence did have a significant relationship with violence during the Second Intifada. Here we are reporting only the impact of past violence on the relationship between trade changes and conflict, not the direct impact on conflict.

References

Acemoglu, D., and J. Robinson. 2006. *The Economic Origins of Dictatorship and Democracy*. Cambridge, UK: Cambridge University Press.

Alesina, A., A. Dzevleeschauwer, R. Wacziarg, S. Kurlat, and W. Easterly. 2003. "Fractionalization." *Journal of Economic Growth* 8 (2): 155–94.

Anderson, K., M. Kurzweil, W. Martin, D. Sandri, and E. Valenzuela. 2008. "Measuring Distortions to Agricultural Incentives, Revisited." Policy Research Working Paper 4612, World Bank.

Angrist, J., and A. D. Kugler. 2008. "Rural Windfall or a New Resource Curse? Coca, Income, and Civil Conflict in Colombia." *The Review of Economics and Statistics* 90 (2): 191–215.

Atkin, D., and D. Donaldson. 2014. "Who's Getting Globalized? The Size and Implications of Intranational Trade Costs." Mimeo.

Bazzi, S., and C. Blattman. 2014. "Economic Shocks and Conflict: Evidence from Commodity Prices." *American Economic Journal: Macroeconomics*.

Bellows, J., and E. Miguel. 2009. "War and Local Collective Action in Sierra Leone." *Journal of Public Economics* 93 (11–12): 1144–57.

Berman, N., and M. Couttenier. 2014. "External Shocks, Internal Shots: The Geography of Civil Conflicts." CEPR Discussion Paper 9895.

Besley, T., and T. Persson. 2008. "The Incidence of Civil War: Theory and Evidence." Mimeo.

Bhagwati, J. N. 1978. *Foreign Trade Regimes and Economic Development: Anatomy and Consequences of Exchange Control Regimes*. Cambridge, MA: Ballinger.

Blair, R., C. Blattman, and A. Hartman. 2012. "Patterns of Conflict and Cooperation in Liberia (Part 2): Prospects for Conflict Forecasting and Early Warning." Yale University and IPA, Mimeo.

Blattman, C., and E. Miguel. 2010. "Civil War." *Journal of Economic Literature* 48: 3–57.

Blimes, R. J. 2006. "The Indirect Effect of Ethnic Heterogeneity on the Likelihood of Civil War Onset." *Journal of Conflict Resolution* 50, 4.

Brosio, G., and R. Singh. 2014. "Revenue Sharing of Natural Resources: A Review of International Practices." World Bank, Mimeo.

Bruekner and Gradstein. 2014. "Income Growth, Ethnic Polarization, and Political Risk." *Journal of Comparative Economics*, forthcoming.

Buhaug, H., L.-E. Cederman, and K. S. Gleditsch. 2011. "Square Pegs in Round Holes: Inequalities, Grievances, and Civil War." Mimeo.

Buhaug, H., and K. S. Gleditsch. 2008. "Contagion or Confusion? Why Conflicts Cluster in Space." *International Studies Quarterly* 52 (2): 215–33.

Carter, B. L., and R. Bates. 2012. "Public Policy, Price Shocks, and Civil War in Developing Countries." Georgetown University, Mimeo.

Caselli, F., and A. Tesei. 2013. "Resource Windfalls, Political Regimes, and Political Stability." Mimeo.

Cederman, L., L. Girardin, and K. S. Gleditsch. 2009. "Ethnonationalist Triads: Assessing the Influence of Kin Groups on Civil Wars." *World Politics* 61 (3): 403–37.

Collier, P., and A. Hoffler. 2004. "Greed and Grievance in Civil War." *Oxford Economic Papers* 56 (4): 563–96.

Corden, W. M. 1971. *The Theory of Protection*. Oxford: Clarendon Press.

Easterly, W., and R. Levine. 1997. "Africa's Growth Tragedy: Policies and Ethnic Divisions." *Quarterly Journal of Economics* 112 (4): 1203–50.

Fearon, J. 2005. "Primary Commodity Exports and Civil War." *Journal of Conflict Resolution* 49 (4): 483–507.

Fearon, J., and D. Laitin. 2003. "Ethnicity, Insurgency, and Civil War." *American Political Science Review* 97 (1): 75–90.

Gleditsch, K. S. 2007. "Transnational Dimensions of Civil War." *Journal of Peace Research* 44: 293–309.

Gomes, J. F. 2011. "The Political Economy of the Maoist Conflict in India: An Empirical Analysis." Mimeo.

Hidalgo, F. D., S. Naidu, S. Nichter, and N. Richardson. 2010. "Economic Determinants of Land Invasions." *The Review of Economics and Statistics* 92 (3): 505–23.

Hull, P., and M. Imai. 2013. "Economic Shocks and Civil Conflict: Evidence from Foreign Interest Rate Movements." *Journal of Development Economics* 103: 77–89.

Ianchovichina, E., J. Loening, and C. Wood. 2012. "How Vulnerable Are Arab Countries to Global Food Price Shocks?" Policy Research Working Paper 6018, World Bank.

International Crisis Group. 2010. "Dangerous Little Stones: Diamonds in the Central African Republic." Africa Report 167.

Ivanic, M., and W. Martin. 2013. "World Food Price Rises and the Poor 2006–12: A Slow Food Price Crisis?" World Bank, Mimeo.

Ksoll, C., R. Macchiavello, and A. Morjaria. 2010. "The Effect of Ethnic Violence of an Export-Oriented Industry." Mimeo.

Losch, B. 2002. "Global Restructuring and Liberalization: Côte d'Ivoire and the End of the International Cocoa Market." *Journal of Agrarian Change* 2 (2): 206–27.

Maystadt, J.-F. 2008. "Does Inequality Make Us Rebel? A Revisited Theoretical Model Applied to South Mexico." Households in Conflict Network Working Paper 41.

Miaari, S., A. Zussman, and N. Zussman. 2014. "Employment Restrictions and Political Violence in the Israeli-Palestinian Conflict." *Journal of Economic Behavior and Organization* 101 (May): 24–44.

Miguel, E., S. Satyanath, and E. Sergenti. 2004. "Economic Shocks and Civil Conflict: An Instrumental Variables Approach." *Journal of Political Economy* 112 (4): 725–53.

Minot, N. 2011. "Transmission of World Food Price Changes to Markets in Sub-Saharan Africa." IFPRI Discussion Paper 1059.

Montalvo, J. G., and M. Reynal-Querol. 2005. "Ethnic Polarization, Potential Conflict, and Civil Wars." *American Economic Review* 95 (3).

Nepal, M., B. K. Bohara, and K. Gawande. 2011. "More Inequality, More Killings: The Maoist Insurgency in Nepal." *American Journal of Political Science* 55: 886–906.

NNoli, O. 2003. "Ethnic Violence in Nigeria: An Historical Perspective." Indiana University, Bloomington. http://www.indiana.edu/~workshop/papers/nnoli_021003.pdf.

Persson, T., and G. Tabellini. 2003. *The Economic Effects of Constitutions*. Boston, MA: MIT Press.

Robinson, J. A., D. Acemoglu, and S. Johnson. 2003. "An African Success Story: Botswana." In *In Search of Prosperity: Analytic Narratives on Economic Growth*, edited by D. Rodrik, 80–119. Princeton, NJ: Princeton University Press.

World Bank. 2011. *World Development Report 2011: Conflict, Security and Development.* Washington, DC: World Bank.

———. 2014. "Lebanon Economic Monitor, Spring 2014." World Bank, Washington, DC and Beirut.

CHAPTER 3

How Trade Policy Could Ease Tensions in Fragile Countries

The first two chapters showed that international trade matters for civil conflict.[1] This general finding confirms growing evidence gathered over the past decade that changes in prices and incomes are important determinants of civil conflict (Blattman and Miguel 2010; Miguel, Satyanath, and Sergenti 2004). It also complements the evidence on the importance of trade for inter-state conflicts (Martin, Mayer, and Thoenig 2012).

Part of the reason why trade is important for civil conflicts is that it is the largest external flow in fragile countries, which are the ones most exposed to the risk of conflict. But this report shows that its importance extends beyond that. For example, trade enables countries to monetize their natural resources, which in fragile countries often represent the bulk of economic resources. This affects the potential for conflict by raising the economic value involved in gaining hold of these resources through violence, and also by providing funds to the government which can be used to repress or buy off rebel groups.

Trade also affects real incomes and thus individuals' opportunity costs of engaging in violence. In many fragile countries, open trade regimes have provided essential consumption goods to households, especially food. Moreover, open trade regimes increase real incomes by improving efficiency and providing opportunities for exports. On the other hand, an open trade regime can also quickly transmit the effects of international price swings onto households. In the context of fragile countries, sharp, adverse changes in the prices households face on the goods they consume or produce can increase the potential for conflict.

The natural question that follows is how to use these findings to inform the policy debate, and trade policy in particular. This chapter attempts to do this by focusing on a narrow but arguably fundamental policy objective in fragile countries, i.e. preventing civil conflict or quelling existing ones. As argued by scholars such as Collier (2008) and del Castillo (2011), this should be the guiding principle of engagement in conflict affected and post-conflict countries. This is not the first time that the World Bank has explored how policies affect conflict.

Illustrious antecedents include Collier et al. (2003) and more recently the 2011 World Development Report on conflict, security, and development (World Bank 2011). However, this is the first policy analysis that explicitly focuses on trade.

The policy ideas discussed are not only directed to domestic policy makers. Whenever possible, we consider how the international community, including the World Bank, can assist countries to formulate policies that take into account the risk of conflict linked to trade. This is important also in light of IEG (2013b), which stresses the need for the World Bank to better tailor its assistance to fragility and conflict contexts.[2]

As documented in this report, the drivers of conflict differ across countries. Moreover, governments, particularly in fragile countries, have different degrees of capacity. In this sense, the options discussed below have to be interpreted more as general directions that need to be tailored to the local situation, rather than as policy prescriptions. Similarly, this policy discussion does not attempt to evaluate the feasibility of the various policy options, which would require a country-specific political economy analysis. The absence of such an analysis does not, however, detract from the value of the general directions discussed below.

Trade Policies in Fragile Countries Must Take into Account the Implications for Conflict

Trade policies in fragile countries need to be compatible with the objective of supporting political stability. This requires an understanding of the relationship between trade and conflict, which our analysis suggests can be adequately developed only at the level of the country or below. That is, the differences in this relationship among countries are so great that cross-country analysis is an unreliable guide to country-specific advice. For example, our analysis suggests that point-source commodities, like oil or gas, are the exports that most frequently become drivers of conflict. However, this is true to a different extent in different contexts, and even across time. In Nigeria, the estimated relationship between oil production and conflict was positive for most of the period studied, but then turned not significant for the period following the amnesty agreement with rebel groups. By contrast, in the West Bank and Gaza changes in export revenues were an important driver of conflict, despite the absence of point-source commodity exports.

A growing literature, including this report, shows the data required to analyze the relationship between trade and conflict at the country level. These data are essential to develop a framework to monitor the implications for the risk of conflict of both trade policies and trade-related changes. Such a framework should fulfill at least two main objectives:

a. It should identify the changes in trade that would matter most for the country's stability. For example, it would identify the subset of traded goods (and services) that are most relevant for the economy and the types of economic changes (e.g. international price swings, changes in trade policies in the country concerned or its trading partners) that affect the domestic prices of these goods (and services).

b. The framework should also help assess the likely distribution of gains and losses across different groups within the country as a result of the change in trade. This assessment, along with a political economy analysis, could help policy makers understand to what extent the losers may be willing and capable of destabilizing the country (or areas of it) following an adverse change in trade flows.

A monitoring framework of this type would be particularly important for those countries most exposed to the risk of conflict due to changes in trade flows. These countries are not necessarily limited to those in the World Bank's FCS list; nor is the inclusion in the FCS list sufficient to be considered exposed to this risk. As the IEG (2013b) argues, the World Bank's definition of fragility does not always adequately take into account indicators of conflict, violence, and political risk.

In this respect, an empirical analysis like in chapter 2 can identify the conditions that increase the conflict risk connected to trade changes. Important conditions that affect the relationship between trade changes and conflict include the presence of conflict in neighboring countries, ethnic divisions, a recent history of past conflicts, and weak and/or corrupt government institutions. As many of the countries fitting this profile lack adequate human and financial resources, technical assistance from organizations like the World Bank may be important to putting such a monitoring framework in place.

Manage Receipts from Commodity Exports in a Conflict-Sensitive Way

Previous evidence across and within countries (Bellows and Miguel 2009; Dube and Vargas 2013; Lin and Michaels 2013; Maystadt et al. 2014) as well as the analysis in the previous chapters, suggest that exports of point-source commodities substantially raise the risk of conflict. In many countries, these exports represent the bulk of the state's revenues or of the local area's resources. Thus their value is often the prize which the different parties fight over.

The way in which point-source commodity export revenues are managed is thus a key factor in determining their effect on conflict risk.[3] According to the evidence in chapter 2, that is especially the case in countries located in unstable regions, with a recent history of conflict, and with weak governance. In particular, the evidence suggests two general principles that should reduce the conflict inducing effect of point-source exports.

First, the discretion of the central or local governments in managing these resource revenues should not be absolute. Effective limitations on the spending of revenues by government, and procedures to ensure the transparency of such expenditures, are essential for two reasons. First, they can reduce the potential for governments to discriminate against some groups, and thus limit the resentments and disputes that can result in civil conflict. In addition, if it is possible, for example through international arrangements, to reduce government access to resource revenues, then the incentive to rebel in order to control these revenues is reduced. This perspective is consistent with the analysis in chapter 2, which shows that increases in the prices of point-source commodity exports are associated with a larger increase in conflict where government accountability is low. Often windfall increases in oil or minerals prices are captured by the government, state-owned entities, or national-resource companies, which have total discretion on how to spend such resources. This appears to have been the case in the Republic of South Sudan, where the renewal of oil exports to Sudan in April 2013 was followed by increased political violence, which eventually triggered the current civil war. On the other hand, the development of a transparent and accountable oil revenue management system was associated with a peaceful post-independence political transition in oil dependent Timor-Leste (see box 1.3).

Second, transferring part of the revenues from point-source commodities to the producing areas can reduce the risk of conflict. This can be deduced from the results of recent studies. First, federal systems, which are typically more inclined to reward natural resources–producing areas (Brosio and Singh 2014), are less subject to conflict risk from trade-related changes. Second, conflicts over extractive resources occur overwhelmingly in producing areas, as also confirmed by Dube and Vargas (2013), Berman et al. (2014), and Maystadt et al. (2014). Third, transferring resources to local militant groups helped reduce the intensity of the conflict in the oil-producing Niger Delta, at least in the short run. Producing areas can be rewarded by channeling resources through individuals, organizations, or subnational governments. Besides conflict prevention, this transfer is also justified from an economic standpoint as compensation for the environmental degradation and socioeconomic evils generated locally by natural resource extraction (Brosio and Singh 2014).

These principles may not apply when nonstate actors (e.g. local rebel groups) rather than the state control the extraction and the sale of the natural resources. In those instances, the revenues are usually employed to fund the fighting. Thus, other strategies that are not completely dependent on the government may have to be implemented to break the link between increased revenues and conflict (see below).

Using these principles in formulating policies to manage point-source commodity revenues requires adapting them to the local context. Examples of policy options in line with these principles include the following:

a. *Increase the transparency of the flow of revenues from extractive commodities.* Domestic policies could help achieve that objective, for example by centralizing the collection of the revenues into a single account under the authority of a Ministry (typically the Ministry of Finance) as suggested by Haysome and Kane (2009). In addition, a number of international initiatives help governments to enhance transparency. The Extractive Industries Transfer Initiative (EITI), a global coalition of governments, companies, and civil society helping to ensure the disclosure of taxes and other payments made by oil, gas, and mining companies to governments, is perhaps best known in this respect. Recent years have seen a flurry of other global initiatives with similar aims, such as the Publish What You Pay (PWYP) network, the Kimberley Process (KP) on the diamond sector, and the Conflict Free Gold Standard on the gold sector. By enhancing the transparency around the flow of these revenues, these initiatives can also make it more difficult for nonstate actors to use the sale of extractive commodities to fund their own fighting.

b. *Transfer a percentage of extractive commodities' rents to citizens.* This option—perhaps best known as Direct Dividend Payments (DDPs)—has been gaining momentum in recent years among scholars (see Gillies 2010; Moss 2011; Devarajan and Giugale 2012; and Devarajan et al. 2013). It has also been implemented especially at the subnational states, notably in the states of Alaska (USA) and Alberta (Canada). It has not yet gained much traction in developing countries but its proponents argue that DDPs can maximize the direct effects of resource revenues on poverty reduction and improve the accountability and the efficiency of public spending through enhanced scrutiny by citizens. For example, Devarajan et al. (2013) estimate that in Equatorial Guinea the per person distribution of just 10 percent of resource revenues through a DDP would be one and a half times larger than the money the average poor person needs to exit poverty. According to their proponents, DDPs would also help establish a stronger fiscal contract between the citizens and their government, by increasing citizens' incentives to oversee how the government manages natural resources' revenues, and possibly by taxing back some of the DDPs.

While not initially proposed with conflict in mind, DDPs have two potentially important benefits in the quest for conflict prevention in resource rich countries. First, if citizens benefit directly from the revenues, their incentive to oppose any attempt by government to regain full control over resource revenues (e.g. by eliminating the DDPs) would be higher. Similarly, citizens benefiting from DDPs may oppose attempts by nonstate actors to gain control of extractive resources. Second, as argued by Devarajan and Giugale (2013), greater citizens' involvement could strengthen oversight of the spending of resource revenues in general. That could limit the state's ability to capture the natural resource rents and thus the incentives for fighting to appropriate the resources.

This option could also be combined with the principle of rewarding areas where resources are extracted. In that case the amount of the direct transfer to the citizens may be differentiated on the basis of their location of residence, with citizens from producing areas receiving a higher amount than the others.[4]

c. *Create a financial vehicle outside the direct control of the government to channel part of the resource revenues.* This is another way to limit the ability of the government to capture point-source commodity rents. The most common of such vehicles is the Sovereign Wealth Fund (SWF), which have been successfully established by various resource rich countries, such as Norway, Timor-Leste, Brazil, Mexico, Chile, and Colombia. Some of these funds have helped improve the long-term returns of extractive revenues, smooth the business cycle, and enhance transparency in the spending of revenues from natural resources. The high quality of Timor-Leste's SWF has also been associated with a peaceful post-independence transition (box 1.3).

However, the record of SWFs in furthering development is mixed. Several SWFs operate with no disclosure, limiting their accountability and increasing the risk of corruption (Revenue Watch Institute 2013). In addition, saving resource revenues through an SWF may not be the optimal strategy in many developing countries, especially those with high levels of poverty where these revenues may be more profitably channeled toward investments and consumption. IEG (2011) points out that in Timor-Leste itself the management of oil revenues—in line with the World Bank's advice—favored high levels of savings and placed too little emphasis on short-term interventions that would have yielded immediate benefits to the population.

d. *Use resource revenues to placate rebel groups in the producing areas.* The evidence in chapter 1 suggests that the use of oil revenues for the DDRR program for the militant groups appears to have been effective in reducing violence in the Niger Delta, at least in the short run. The evidence in favor of this strategy remains thin, and even in Nigeria it has been criticized for failing to treat the root causes of conflict, and for providing incentives toward "warlordism" (Sayne 2013). Indeed, without parallel policies addressing the deep determinants of conflict (according to Joab-Peterside et al. [2012], youth unemployment, ineffective and corrupt public institutions, human and ecological insecurity), civil unrest is likely to resume and the program risks ending up promoting "warlordism." However, the evidence supporting the success of the alternative—usually the preferred option by autocracies (Cotet and Tsui 2013)—of using extractive commodity revenues to increase armed repression is also pretty limited. For example, in Nigeria heightened military repression in the oil-producing areas before the 2009 agreement was not associated with a reduction in violence. In fact, the military repression may have even contributed to the escalation of violence (Asuni 2009; Rosenau et al. 2009). Similarly, increased foreign military assistance in Colombia was ineffective in reducing guerrilla attacks and even increased paramilitary attacks (Dube and Naidu 2013). The decision as to whether to attempt to reach agreement with, or to fight, militant groups is ultimately a political one. Each of these strategies needs to be accompanied by attempts to address the root causes of the conflicts for a sustainable peace.

Again, the international community could be instrumental in helping countries in the identification and the implementation of the most effective policy options in some of these areas. First, it could provide support to the government in developing cost-benefit analyses of the alternative options. Second, it could offer technical assistance in the actual implementation of the policies, as the World Bank did in the establishment of Timor-Leste's petroleum fund. Third, it could exert pressure on governments when the most effective option for conflict prevention is not in line with the policy makers' interests.

Protect Producers, Consumers, and Workers from Adverse Trade Shocks

The evidence from Nigeria and the West Bank and Gaza presented in chapter 1 confirms that adverse changes in trade flows can increase conflict intensity. By reducing real incomes of consumers, producers, and workers, such changes reduced the opportunity cost of fighting. That is also the evidence emerging from other within-country studies (e.g. Berman and Couttenier 2014; Dube and Vargas 2013; Maystadt and Ecker 2014). On the other hand, the cross-country evidence is inconclusive in this respect (see for example the evidence in chapter 1 and in Bazzi and Blattman 2014).

Where adverse trade changes increase conflict via the opportunity cost channel, protecting the real incomes of consumers, producers, and workers should be a priority. A variety of policy options exist to do this, for example targeted transfers, public works programs, price subsidies, and temporary trade insulation.

All of these policies have strengths and weaknesses, and the identification of the right policy tool in each context is beyond the scope of this discussion. However, the evidence suggests that targeted transfers appear to be particularly useful in counteracting the losses by households as a result of an adverse trade change (Anderson, Ivanic, and Martin 2013; Attanasio et al. 2013). Furthermore, it is important that the policies adopted avoid, to the extent possible, impeding adjustment to the changes in relative prices caused by changes in trade. From this perspective, targeted transfers (as well as public works programs) may be preferable to price subsidies and temporary trade insulation.[5] In general, however, effective safety nets are difficult to develop. Providing protection to all possible losers is costly, and proper targeting is inherently difficult, especially in fragile countries.

The international community could help fund programs that fragile countries use to protect their citizens from adverse trade changes. One relevant antecedent in this respect is the Global Food Crisis Response Program (GFRP), which was set up by the World Bank to help countries address the immediate needs arising from the international food price hike in 2007–08. The GFRP supported 35 countries, with Sub-Saharan Africa accounting for about 60 percent of funding. Most of the short-term assistance was to the agricultural sector (via input subsidy and distribution operations to increase food supply) and to social safety nets (in-kind transfers and public works programs). A recent independent evaluation considered the program effective in helping poor countries deal with the immediate consequence of the price crisis (IEG 2013a).[6] It may be useful to think about a similar international shock absorption fund to help fragile countries deal with adverse trade shocks, including international price swings.

Promote Trade with Neighbors

The previous analysis suggests that promoting trade with a country's neighbors reduces the risk of conflict, or at least its intensity and duration. This trade is particularly effective in preventing conflict when it occurs under an RTA. While this result is novel in the empirical literature, it is consistent with the idea that a high volume of trade between two neighbors A and B increases the costs to A of a conflict in B, thus reducing the likelihood that A would intervene to foment civil conflict in B (and vice versa). It is also in line with the idea that trade may raise the level of trust between the peoples of neighboring countries (Rohner, Thoenig, and Zilibotti 2013).

Trade policy as well as trade facilitation can help foster these trade relations among neighbors. Reducing tariff and nontariff barriers is a necessary step in this direction. There is abundant evidence of the existence of high policy barriers to trade, especially between fragile countries. Such barriers even constrain trade in basic food staples between sub-Saharan African neighbors (World Bank 2012). Similarly, policy barriers to trade between neighbors in other major conflict-affected regions, the Middle East and North Africa and South Asia, are particularly high.

While necessary, efficient trade policy is not sufficient to stimulate trade between neighboring fragile countries, most of which are marred by particularly poor transit, logistics, and transport infrastructure systems (see the analysis in chapter 1). Improving the whole trade facilitation system is therefore crucial to increase trade between neighbors in conflict prone areas. That is part of the objective, for example, of the large program of assistance of the World Bank to the Great Lakes region, where increasing cross-border trade is considered as contributing to regional stability. Similarly, the African Union (AU) established the African Union Border Program in 2007 with a view to preventing conflict by promoting cross-border cooperation and trade (World Bank 2011). Unfortunately, no evidence is available so far on the effectiveness of this initiative for conflict prevention.

Support Labor-Intensive Exports

The evidence from the Israeli-Palestinian conflict presented in this report suggests that the main channel through which exports (of nonpoint-source commodities) affect conflict is through employment. This is consistent with the finding that changes in employment in Palestine had an important effect on conflict intensity (Miaari, Zussman, and Zussman 2014) as well as with recent theoretical contributions (Dal Bó and Dal Bó 2011, 2012).[7]

This finding suggests that promoting labor-intensive export sectors in fragile countries may help reduce conflict intensity and risk. There are two main (mutually reinforcing) ways to promote labor-intensive exports. First, a country can improve its market access in labor-intensive sectors in its main trading partners. This access is essentially dependent on the trade policy of a country's trading partners. As far as tariffs are concerned, the data of Carpenter and Lendle (2011) show that there is still much room to improve fragile countries' preferential access to the main markets.[8] Among the 25 developing countries with the largest preference margins for their exports in the main importers, only three are FCS (Haiti, Afghanistan, and Nepal). Reducing nontariff barriers is likely to provide even further mileage in increasing this access (Hoekman and Nicita 2011).

Market access for developing countries is even more restricted in trade in services, especially via the temporary movement of natural persons (Saez 2013). This type of service export (mode 4 services trade in WTO terminology) has a direct impact on employment. Expanding market access via mode 4 in labor-importing countries could yield direct employment benefits for fragile countries.

The second way to enhance the employment effect of exports is by increasing the relative competitiveness of fragile countries' exports, particularly in labor-intensive sectors. This requires a broad set of interventions to improve trade connectivity and firms' productivity (Reis and Farole 2012). In conflict-affected and post-conflict environments, both areas are usually particularly deficient (see the evidence in chapter 1 on the poor performance of fragile countries in trade facilitation), mainly due to the destruction and insecurity caused by the conflict.

The international community has tried to address these constraints. One example is the Conflict Affected States in Africa (CASA) initiative by the International Finance Corporation, which specifically focuses on post-conflict reconstruction.[9] By providing long-term private sector development support, the initiative helps countries address constraints that stifle economic recovery, such as poor government institutional capacity, weak business associations, weak basic infrastructure, and the deterioration of financial services. One approach to improving the efficiency of export production in fragile countries is to develop special economic zones. The idea behind it is that in conflict-affected countries, it should be easier and more effective to achieve international competitiveness for firms in a concentrated environment than in the whole country.[10] While this approach could be effective in promoting competitiveness for a subset of producers, the evidence suggests that the implementation challenges are often daunting (Farole and Akinci 2011).

Build Long-Term Conflict Resilience

The policies that we have so far focused on can be implemented over a relatively short time horizon. This perspective is intrinsic to the report's focus on how to use trade, which is by its nature fast changing, to prevent conflict. However, the analysis in the report also points to the need to modify a country's structural characteristics to build resilience to changes in trade flows. In chapter 2 we point to several long-term conditions that make conflict more sensitive to trade-related changes. The level of grievances and institutional capacity appear particularly important.

Countries may need to focus on a number of areas to reduce grievances. It is essential to achieve some resolution of the tensions arising from past conflicts, both because countries with a recent past of civil conflict are more likely to fall back into conflict in general (World Bank 2011), and because a history of conflict exacerbates the tendency to react to adverse trade changes through violence. Reducing interpersonal economic inequality and tackling ethnic divisions are also priorities to build conflict resilience to trade-related changes.

The analysis also underscores the importance of accountable and honest government institutions to build resilience to changes in trade flows. In addition, it suggests that federal political systems are more resilient to such changes than central systems, probably because the former are better equipped than the latter to respond to the needs of the regions within a country. Clearly, the governments' responsiveness to tensions at the subnational level is likely to be important for stability.

Building these conditions requires a longer term horizon than is usually adopted by a government legislature. Yet investing in them is also likely to be necessary to permanently break the conflict trap.

Notes

1. The concept of conflict in this chapter refers to both conflict risk (for fragile countries not currently in conflict) and conflict intensity (for those where one or more civil conflicts are ongoing).

2. In particular, the IEG evaluation points out that the World Bank is most responsive to FCS in the immediate aftermath of conflict, while the Bank's effectiveness in the medium term has been lower because of a lack of proper understanding of the countries' drivers of conflict.

3. Note that we do not discuss the optimal fiscal instruments to extract revenues from natural resources exports, nor the issue of assigning the ownership of natural resources and the power to regulate their exploitation. These issues are important in determining the size of revenues extractable from the natural resources endowment as well as the political economy of the distribution of the resources. However, the management of the revenues appears to be the really important issue shaping the way resource revenues may affect conflict risk (see Brosio and Singh 2014 for an extensive treatment of the optimal fiscal instruments and Haysome and Kane 2009 for a discussion of the other issues).

4. That may also require a first allocation of the resources across subnational levels of government. See Brosio and Singh (2014) for a discussion on the options for such an allocation.

5. See Do, Levchenko, and Ravallion (2013) for an alternative view suggesting trade insulation, such as export restrictions, as potentially preferable options to social protection.

6. The evaluation highlights five lessons that may be important for any future such initiative (IEG 2013a). First, a detailed strategic framework for crisis response is necessary but not sufficient for the effectiveness of interventions. Second, the expansion in the scale of operations requires commensurate enhancement of administrative budgets. Third, owing to the small amount of additional funding made available, many countries received only modest assistance that could not have had significant crisis-mitigating impact. Fourth, the effectiveness of the assistance depends critically on

adequate analytical work and staff resources. Finally, for short-term responses to any types of crises, having social safety net systems in place before a crisis hits is key to protecting vulnerable households and individuals.

7. This evidence notwithstanding, a note of caution is in order. The empirical basis on the effect of employment generation on conflict is still very thin. A recent systematic review identifies just seven relevant studies, the majority of which either present anecdotal evidence or are based on secondary literature reviews (Holmes et al. 2013).

8. The exporter-level data do not distinguish between sectors in terms of their labor intensity.

9. See http://www.ifc.org/wps/wcm/connect/region__ext_content/regions/sub-saharan +africa/advisory+services/strategicinitiatives/casa.

10. Among other countries, this approach has been tried most recently in Haiti, where a SEZ was started in 2012 mainly to process exports for the U.S. market.

References

Anderson, K., M. Ivanic, and W. Martin. 2013. "Food Price Spikes, Price Insulation and Poverty." World Bank, Mimeo.

Asuni, J. B. 2009. "Blood Oil in the Niger Delta." United States Institute for Peace Special Report 229.

Attanasio, O., V. Di Maro, V. Lechene, and D. Phillips. 2013. "Welfare Consequences of Food Prices Increases: Evidence from Rural Mexico." *Journal of Development Economics* 104: 136–51.

Bazzi, S., and C. Blattman. 2014. "Economic Shocks and Conflict: Evidence from Commodity Prices." *American Economic Journal: Macroeconomics*.

Bellows, J., and E. Miguel. 2009. "War and Local Collective Action in Sierra Leone." *Journal of Public Economics* 93 (11–12): 1144–57.

Berman, N., and M. Couttenier. 2014. "External Shocks, Internal Shots: The Geography of Civil Conflicts." CEPR Discussion Paper 9895.

Berman, N., M. Couttenier, D. Rohner, and M. Thoenig. 2014. "This Mine Is Mine! How Minerals Fuel Conflicts in Africa." OxCarre Research Paper 141.

Blattman, C., and E. Miguel. 2010. "Civil War." *Journal of Economic Literature* 48: 3–57.

Brosio, G., and R. Singh. 2014. "Revenue Sharing of Natural Resources: A Review of International Practices." World Bank, Mimeo.

Carpenter, T., and A. Lendle. 2011. "How Preferential Is World Trade?" CTEI Working Paper, The Graduate Institute, Geneva.

Collier, P. 2008. "Post-Conflict Economic Policy." In *Building States to Build Peace*, edited by C. T. Call. Boulder, CO: Lynne Rienner.

Collier, P., V. L. Elliott, H. Hegre, A. Hoeffler, M. Reynal-Querol, and N. Sambanis. 2003. *Breaking the Conflict Trap: Civil War and Development Policy.* Washington, DC: World Bank and Oxford University Press.

Cotet, A. M., and K. K. Tsui. 2013. "Oil and Conflict: What Does the Cross Country Evidence Really Show?" *American Economic Journal: Macroeconomics* 5 (1): 49–80.

Dal Bó, E., and P. Dal Bó. 2011. "Workers, Warriors and Criminals: Social Conflict in General Equilibrium." *Journal of the European Economic Association* 9 (4).

————. 2012. "Conflict and Policy in General Equilibrium: Insights from a Standard Trade Model." In M. R. Garfinkel and S. Skaperdas (eds.), *The Oxford Handbook of the Economics of Peace and Conflict*. New York: Oxford University Press.

del Castillo, G. 2011. *The Economics of Peace: Five Rules for Effective Reconstruction*. Special Report 286, U.S. Institute of Peace.

Devarajan, S., and M. Giugale. 2012. "The Case for Direct Transfers of Resource Rents in Africa." World Bank, Mimeo.

Devarajan, S., M. Giugale, H. Ehrhart, T. M. Le, and H. M. Nguyen. 2013. "The Case for Direct Transfers of Resource Revenues in Africa." CGD Working Paper 333.

Do, Q. T., A. Levchenko, and M. Ravallion. 2013. "Trade Insulation as Social Protection." Policy Research Working Paper 6448, World Bank.

Dube, O., and S. Naidu. 2013. "Bases, Bullets and Ballots: The Effect of U.S. Military Aid on Political Conflict in Colombia." Mimeo.

Dube, O., and J. Vargas. 2013. "Commodity Price Shocks and Civil Conflict: Evidence from Colombia." *Review of Economic Studies* 80 (4): 1384–21.

Farole, T., and G. Akinci. 2011. *Special Economic Zones: Progress, Emerging Challenges, and Future Directions*. Directions in Development, World Bank.

Gillies, A. 2010. "Giving Money Away? The Politics of Direct Distribution in Resource-Rich States." Center for Global Development Working Paper 231.

Haysome, N., and S. Kane. 2009. "Negotiating Natural Resources for Peace: Ownership, Control and Wealth-Sharing." Briefing Paper, Center for Humanitarian Dialogue.

Hoekman, B., and A. Nicita. 2011. "Trade Policy, Trade Costs, and Developing Country Trade." *World Development* 39 (12): 2069–79.

Holmes, R., A. McCord, and J. Hagen-Zanker, with G. Bergh and F. Zanker. 2013. *What Is the Evidence on the Impact of Employment Creation on Stability and Poverty Reduction in Fragile States: A Systematic Review*. London: ODI.

IEG. 2011. *Timor-Leste Country Program Evaluation, 2000–2010*. Washington, DC: Independent Evaluation Group.

————. 2013a. *The World Bank Group and the Global Food Crisis: An Evaluation of the World Bank Group Response*. Washington, DC: Independent Evaluation Group.

————. 2013b. *World Bank Group Assistance to Low-Income Fragile and Conflict-Affected States: An Independent Evaluation*. Independent Evaluation Group, Washington, DC.

Joab-Peterside, S., D. Porter, and M. Watts. 2012. "Rethinking Conflict in the Niger Delta: Understanding Conflict Dynamics, Justice and Security." Working Paper 26, Berkeley: University of California.

Lin, Y-H., and G. Michaels. 2013. "Do Giant Oilfield Discoveries Fuel Internal Armed Conflicts?" LSE, Mimeo.

Martin, P., T. Mayer, and M. Thoenig. 2012. "The Geography of Conflicts and Regional Trade Agreements." *American Economic Journal: Macroeconomics* 4 (4): 1–35.

Maystadt, J-F., G. De Luca, P. G. Sekeris, J. Ulimwengu, and R. Folledo. 2014. "Mineral Resources and Conflicts in the Democratic Republic of the Congo." *Oxford Economic Papers* 66 (3): 721–49. http://oep.oxfordjournals.org/content/66/3/721.

Maystadt, J.-F., and O. Ecker. 2014. "Extreme Weather and Civil War: Does Drought Fuel Conflict in Somalia through Livestock Price Shocks?" *American Journal of Agricultural Economics*.

Miaari, S., A. Zussman, and N. Zussman. 2014. "Employment Restrictions and Political Violence in the Israeli-Palestinian Conflict." *Journal of Economic Behavior and Organization* 101 (May): 24–44.

Miguel, E., S. Satyanath, and E. Sergenti. 2004. "Economic Shocks and Civil Conflict: An Instrumental Variables Approach." *Journal of Political Economy* 112 (4): 725–53.

Moss, T. 2011. "Oil to Cash: Fighting the Resource Curse through Cash Transfers." CGD Working Paper 237.

Reis, J. G., and T. Farole. 2012. *Trade Competitiveness Diagnostic Toolkit*. Washington, DC: World Bank.

Revenue Watch Institute. 2013. *The 2013 Resource Governance Index*. Washington, DC: Revenue Watch Institute.

Rohner, D., M. Thoenig, and F. Zilibotti. 2013. "War Signals: A Theory of Trade, Trust and Conflict." *Review of Economic Studies* 80 (3): 1114–47.

Rosenau, W., P. Chalk, R. McPherson, M. Parker, and A. Long. 2009. *Corporations and Counterinsurgency*. Rand Corporation.

Saez, S. 2013. *Let Workers Move: Using Bilateral Labor Agreements to Increase Trade in Services*. Washington, DC: World Bank.

Sayne, A. 2013. *What's Next for Security in the Niger Delta?* U.S. Institute for Peace Special Report 333.

World Bank. 2011. *World Development Report 2011: Conflict, Security and Development*. Washington, DC: World Bank.

———. 2012. *Africa Can Help Feed Africa*. Washington, DC: World Bank.

APPENDIX A

Data Issues

Table A.1 Fragile Countries and Territories and Number of Battle Deaths

WB fragile	Avg. deaths 2005–10	Max. death 2005–10	WB non fragile (with high deaths)	Avg. deaths 2005–10	Max. death 2005–10
Afghanistan	4,354	6,238	Sri Lanka	3,420	8,413
Angola	8	25	Pakistan	2,768	6,688
Bosnia and Herzegovina	0	0	India	1,148	1,336
Burundi	104	285	Colombia	538	1,389
Central African Republic	30	86	Russian Federation	437	696
Chad	431	1,250	Philippines	436	692
Comoros	0	0	Algeria	342	499
Congo, Dem. Rep.	585	1,978	Turkey	296	453
Congo, Rep.	0	0	Thailand	159	214
Côte d'Ivoire	0	0	Uganda	157	655
Eritrea	0	0	Ethiopia	150	515
Guinea-Bissau	0	0	Lebanon	129	774
Haiti	0	0	Georgia	104	621
Iraq	2,055	3,658	Iran, Islamic Rep.	78	133
Kiribati	0	0	Nigeria	68	405
Kosovo	0	0	Mali	51	126
Liberia	0	0	Indonesia	36	213
Libya	0	0	Peru	28	56
Marshall Islands	0	0	Niger	23	81
Micronesia, Fed. Sts.	0	0	Tajikistan	16	98
Myanmar	159	232	Ecuador	8	45
Nepal	260	1,104	Saudi Arabia	7	31
Sierra Leone	0	0	Djibouti	6	35
Solomon Islands	0	0	Azerbaijan	4	26
Somalia	1,209	2,158			
Republic of South Sudan	—	—			
Sudan	563	1,029			
Syrian Arab Republic	0	0			
Timor-Leste	0	0			
Togo	0	0			
Tuvalu	0	0			
West Bank and Gaza	NA	NA			
Yemen, Rep.	43	175			
Zimbabwe	0	0			

Sources: World Development Indicators and World Bank 2013.
Note: — = not available. Battle-related deaths are deaths in battle-related conflicts between warring parties in the conflict dyad (two conflict units that are parties to a conflict). The left-hand side of the table comprises the FY13 list of "fragile countries and situations" as classified by the World Bank as: a) having a harmonized average CPIA country rating of 3.2 or less, or b) the presence of a UN and/or regional peace-keeping or peace-building mission during the past 3 years. The right-hand side of the table comprises the list of other countries which have had at least a minor civil conflict (i.e. with at least 25 battle deaths in a year) between 2005 and 2010.

Cross-Country Analysis

We collect data from different sources. For the conflict data we rely on the Uppsala Conflict Data Programme, Peace Research Institute, Oslo (PRIO).[1] Although there are other sources for conflict data (e.g. Fearon and Laitin 2003; Sambanis 2004 and the Correlates of War (COW), Sarkees and Wayman 2010), PRIO has become the key dataset for cross-country analyses of conflict determinants.

While all sources define a civil war as an internal conflict with at least 1,000 battle deaths, there are significant differences in the data concerning the number of fatalities and the criteria used to code the onset of wars, what counts as a war, and how to treat breaks in violence. These differences lead to dramatically differ-ent civil war variables.[2] We are reluctant to test the relationship between trade shocks and conflict using all sources of conflict data, because the differences among them would likely affect the analysis, and could lead to very different results.

Instead, we follow the same practice as Bazzi and Blattman (2014), who base their analysis on the more episodic PRIO and COW measures of conflict. Bazzi and Blattman (2014, p. 13) assert that these databases are most relevant to measuring the impact of commodity price changes on conflict, "as they capture the ebb and flow of incentives for war as incomes rise or fall." We use the PRIO dataset as our main source of conflict data, and only use the COW data for robustness, for three main reasons. First, the PRIO dataset has effec-tively become the standard reference for cross-country studies on the determi-nants of conflict. The majority of the recent studies we have reviewed use only this dataset (e.g. Bruckner and Ciccone 2010; Lin and Michaels 2011; Hull and Imai 2013; Nunn and Qian 2014), while a few use it along with other data sources (e.g., Besley and Persson 2008; Bazzi and Blattman 2014). Second, we have performed independent checks on both datasets and found PRIO to be generally better at identifying civil conflicts than COW.[3] Finally, along with major civil conflicts, PRIO also codes minor conflicts as those above 25 battle deaths per year. We believe these smaller conflicts provide a relevant comple-ment to the more episodic, full-blown civil conflicts. In fact, the problem with estimating the determinants of a rare event as conflict onset strengthens the importance of adding these smaller conflicts to the database (more on this below).

One issue with the major conflict data is that temporary reductions in the yearly number of casualties (i.e. below 1,000) are automatically counted as peace years. For instance, in the Angolan Civil War (1975–2002) the number of fatali-ties was below 1,000 in 1991 and 1995, even though the war was continuing with a large number of yearly casualties. To check the sensitivity of the results to this coding procedure, we also construct an additional conflict variable, which defines peace years in between war years as those with a number of battle-related deaths that fall below 300. The results below for *major conflict onset* are based on this variable although the results are very similar when using the *major conflict onset* from PRIO (results available upon request).

We use various trade variables in the empirical analysis. Two of them (i.e. export and import price indices) rely on a combination of international commodity prices and country-specific trade shares. The former come from data coded by Bazzi and Blattman (2014), who combine price data for 65 commodities from various sources, including the IMF International Financial Statistics (IFS), the U.S. Bureau of Labor Statistics (BLS), Global Financial Data (GFD), and others.[4] We complement data from Bazzi and Blattman (2014) with commodity price data from the World Bank to obtain prices for 73 internationally traded commodities.[5] Using this data we are able to construct the export price index:

$$Px_{it} = ln\left[\left(\prod_j P_{jt}^{exp_{ij,t-k}}\right)^{\frac{1}{\Sigma_j exp_{ij,t-k}}}\right] \tag{A.1}$$

where Px is defined as the log of the geometric average of the international commodity prices (P_{jt}).[6] Each commodity is weighted by its country *i*-specific average value of exports between $t-k$ and $t-2$, where in our case k takes the value of 12 or of 4 (see below). The lagged structure of the export variable ensures the exogeneity of the weights.[7] In addition, the moving average weights can capture changes in the export structure such as large discoveries of oil or gas, which static weights cannot do (Deaton 1995). To compute the weights we construct exports and imports series for the 1962–2010 period at 4-digit (SITC Rev. 2) level by combining the NBER-United Nations Trade data with data from UN COMTRADE. This standard formulation allows the effects of commodity prices on countries to vary according to the commodity's share in a country's export bundle.

In the baseline specification we use "slow moving weights," defined as the average exports of each commodity from $(t-2)$ to $(t-12)$. Lagged averages of 10 years of data ensure a balance between the time invariant weights and "fast moving weights" $(t-2; t-4)$ used by Bazzi and Blattman (2014). This weighting scheme also allows us to control for changes in the export structure without giving excessive weight to changes of the export structure due to temporary shocks.[8]

Two other differences in our index compared to what Bazzi and Blattman (2014) use are important. First, their index is based on percentage changes in the commodities' price. As it turns out, this difference is important for the results.

Second, our baseline index is not scaled by size of the exported commodities compared to gross domestic product (GDP). This is, in principle, a desirable property of such an index (Bazzi and Blattman 2014 reflect the size of exports relative to GDP by multiplying the index by the commodity exports-GDP ratio at the mid-point of the period). Using this scaling does not affect our results in any meaningful way, but it does slightly reduce the number of observations, as GDP data are not available for a few countries in some years (results available upon request).[9] Therefore we do not incorporate this scaling in the index.

In addition to the export price indices, we develop a similar country-specific variable for the import sector:

$$PM_{it} = ln\left[\left(\prod_j P_{jt}^{imp_{ij,t-k}}\right)^{\frac{1}{\Sigma_j imp_{ij,t-k}}}\right] \qquad (A.2)$$

The variable is constructed by using import rather than export data to calculate a weighted average of international commodity prices.

Changes in trade flows arise from other sources than simply changes in international commodity prices. Changes in demand in partner countries may be as important as changes in international prices especially for countries that are not diversified in terms of destination markets. To capture this potential effect, we define a demand shock variable—constructed as a market potential measure—as:

$$MP_{it} = ln\left[\sum_j w_{i,j,t-k} GDP_{jt}\right] \qquad (A.3)$$

where we use nominal GDP (normalized to 100 in 2000) from World Bank (2014) to build an index that is a weighted average of trade partners' GDPs, with each weight w being the lagged average share of country j in total exports of country i over the period defined by $t-k$.

The last trade variable captures the trade relation with neighboring countries and it is defined as:

$$Trade\,Neighbors_{it} = \frac{\Sigma_j border_{ij} * \left(import_{ijt} + export_{ijt}\right)}{\Sigma_j \left(import_{ijt} + export_{ijt}\right)} \qquad (A.4)$$

We use the GeoDist dataset from the Centre d'Études Prospectives et d'Informations Internationales (CEPII) to define contiguous country pairs. The variable *Trade Neighbors* (*TN*) proxies for the level of integration of country i with its neighbors. We expect countries that trade less with neighbors to be at greater risk because the neighboring countries' cost of fueling conflict is lower.

Table A.2 presents the summary statistics of the main variables used in the analysis, while table A.3 lists the interaction terms used in the analysis of how local conditions affect the relationship between changes in trade and conflict.

Table A.2 Summary Statistics, Cross-Country Analysis

Type	Variable	N	Mean	SD	Min	Max
Onset	Civil conflict UCDP/PRIO	3,465	0.044	0.205	0	1
	Major conflict UCDP/PRIO	4,053	0.021	0.144	0	1
	Major conflict (modified) UCDP/PRIO	3,861	0.015	0.123	0	1
	Major conflict COW	3,830	0.027	0.161	0	1
Ending	Civil conflict UCDP/PRIO	1,135	0.1304	0.33689	0	1
	Major conflict UCDP/PRIO	420	0.20714	0.40574	0	1
	Major conflict phasing UCDP/PRIO	559	0.10912	0.31207	0	1
Battle-related deaths	Constructed PRIO	4,300	930.60	4,908	0	150,000
	High PRIO	4,300	1474.4	7,472	0	250,000
	Low PRIO	4,300	306.2	1,802	0	50,000
Trade variables	Px slow moving	4,300	0.068	0.947	−4.332	2.629
	Pm slow moving	4,300	0.072	0.940	−3.308	2.001
	MP slow moving	4,300	0.041	1.002	−1.120	7.404
	Px fast moving	4,300	0.067	0.949	−4.280	2.550
	Pm fast moving	4,298	0.072	0.941	−3.373	1.937
	MP fast moving	4,300	0.040	1.003	−1.103	7.157
Controls	Any conflict since 1946	4,300	0.646	0.478	0	1
	Share trade with border	4,238	0.116	0.156	0	0.891
	Neighbors' conflict (any)	4,300	0.243	0.429	0	1

Sources: Authors' calculations based on UCDP/PRIO and COW data.
Note: UCDP/PRIO refers to Uppsala Conflict Data Program/Peace Research Institute Oslo Conflict Data Set. COW refers to the
Correlates of War Project.

Table A.3 Interaction Variables for the Cross-Country Analysis

Variable	Description	Source
Neighbors		
Neighbors' conflict (any)	Dummy equal to one if there is a conflict in a neighboring country.	PRIO
Share trade neighbors RTA	Share of trade with neighbors with an RTA.	COMTRADE + WTO
Share trade neighbors	Share of trade with neighbors.	COMTRADE
Grievances		
Economic inequality	Dataset derived from the econometric relationship between UTIP-UNIDO, other conditioning variables, and the World Bank's Deininger & Squire dataset.	EHII University of Texas
gini_net	Estimate of Gini index of inequality in equivalized (square root scale) household disposable (post-tax, post-transfer) income, using Luxembourg Income Study data as the standard.	SWIID
gini_market	Estimate of Gini index of inequality in equivalized (square root scale) household market (pre-tax, pre-transfer) income, using Luxembourg Income Study data as the standard.	SWIID
Ethnic fractionalization	The probability that two randomly selected individuals in a country will belong to different ethno-linguistic groups.	Montalvo and Reynal-Querol 2005

table continues next page

Table A.3 Interaction Variables for the Cross-Country Analysis *(continued)*

Variable	Description	Source
Ethnic polarization	How far the distribution of the ethnic groups is from the bipolar distribution (i.e. 1/2, 0, 0, ... 0, 1/2)	Montalvo and Reynal-Querol 2005
Religious fractionalization	The probability that two randomly selected individuals in a country will belong to different religious groups.	Montalvo and Reynal-Querol 2005
Religious polarization	How far the distribution of the religious groups is from the bipolar distribution (i.e. 1/2, 0, 0, ... 0, 1/2)	Montalvo and Reynal-Querol 2005
Any conflict in last 10 yrs	Dummy equal to one if there was a conflict in the last 10 years.	PRIO
Political system		
Elections	Dummy for election in that year.	NELDA
Federal Govt.	Dummy for a government with a federal system.	Institutions and Elections Project
Polity2	Captures the political regime characteristics.	Polity
Parliamentary democracy	Dummy for being a parliamentary (from DPI) democracy (Polity).	DPI + Polity
Programmatic party	Share of the major four political parties with an ideological orientation with respect to economic policy, weighted by number of votes.	DPI
Age of party in office		DPI
Governance		
Law	Strength and impartiality of the legal system.	ICRG
Military	Indicates the degree of military participation in politics.	ICRG
Accountability	A measure of how responsive a government is to its people.	ICRG
Corruption	A measure of the level of corruption.	ICRG
Bureaucratic	Indicates the "strength and quality of the bureaucracy."	ICRG
Composite index	The mean value of the ICRG variables "Corruption," "Law and Order," and "Bureaucracy Quality."	ICRG
Price transmission		
nra_covt	Value of production-weighted average of covered products.	Anderson et al. 2008
nra_cov_o	Value of production-weighted average of covered products.	Anderson et al. 2008

Note: PRIO is the Peace Research Institute, Oslo. ICRG is the International Country Risk Guide. COMTRADE refers to the Commodity Trade Statistics Database. WTO is the World Trade Organization. EHII is the Estimated Household Income Inequality dataset. DPI is the World Bank's Database of Political Institutions. SWIID is the Standardized World Income Inequality Database. NELDA is the National Elections Across Democracy and Autocracy database. Sources are given in the table.

Nigeria

The data on conflict we use in this study is the Version 4 (1997–2013) of ACLED. This version of the data covers all countries on the African continent from 1997. ACLED definitions mainly concern actors and events. ACLED collects and codes reports from the developing world on civil and communal conflicts, militia interactions, violence against civilians, rioting, and protesting. ACLED covers activity that occurs both within and outside the context of a civil war.

The calculation of consumption and production price indices is essential to the model estimation. While there are a number of surveys in Nigeria, we use the Nigeria Living Standards Survey (NLSS) 2003/04. This is the first survey of the income and expenditure patterns of Nigerian households with sufficient data to analyze conflict over time.[10] Before describing the survey itself, we summarize the methodology used in calculating the price indices.

The consumption price index *CI* for state s at time t is constructed as a geometric average of prices weighted by the budget shares (computed from the 2003/04 NLSS):

$$CI_{st} = \left[\Pi_{j=1}^{N} \left(\left(p_{jst} \right)^{Expshr_{sj}^{2003}} \right) \right] \times \frac{\Sigma_{j=1}^{N} Exptot_{sj}^{2003}}{TotExp_{s}^{2003}} \tag{A.5}$$

where p_{jst} is the price of good *j* in state s at time t and *Expshr*^{2003} is the share of *j* in total expenditures in 2003/04 across households in *s* on all the *N* items for which price data are available. In this way the sum of the shares always equal to 1. As we can only match a subset of consumed items with prices (the list of items matched is available on request), we scale this index by the importance of those expenditure items in total household expenditures in the state *TotExp* (the latter term in equation A.5).[11]

The main advantage of the geometric over the arithmetic average is that it allows the index to incorporate some substitution effect across commodities as relative prices change. This type of formulation is common in the literature on commodity prices and conflict (e.g. Arezki and Brückner 2011; Bazzi and Blattman 2014; Calì and Mulabdic 2014).

The domestic price data come from Nigeria's National Bureau of Statistics (NBS), which collects monthly data for 143 food and nonfood items by state in both rural and urban areas. The price data we use covers 2000–10.[12] Our analysis relies on the urban data, assuming that rural prices will be a markup/discounted value of the urban prices. The rural data are not used because the Nigerian classification of the areas into urban and rural has not been updated since 1991, and thus they are not representative of the current division into urban and rural. We use two approaches to determining which price index from the NBS data is matched to which production or consumption item from the household survey. The first is a narrow price match, where the good is matched to price data with exactly the same name. However, the limited number of items in the price data means that relying on a narrow price match alone could exclude potentially important consumption items that have no exact match in the price data. The second approach is a broad price match, where the price of a food crop is also applied to products which are complements of, or derived from, that food crop (e.g. the price of cassava is used for its extract gavi).[13] The value of the scaling factor for both consumption and production indices by state, for the narrow and broad match, are available on request.

We construct the production price index in a similar fashion:

$$PI_{st} = \left[\Pi_{j=1}^{K} \left(\left(p_{jst} \right)^{Prodshr_{sj}^{2003}} \right) \right] \times \frac{\Sigma_{j=1}^{K} Prodtot_{sj}^{2003}}{TotInc_{s}^{2003}} \qquad (A.6)$$

Where *Prodshr* are the shares of *j* in all *K* products for which price data are available (thus the shares sum to 1) and *TotInc* is the total household income from all sources in the state.

Because each commodity price may refer to a different unit of measurement, we normalize the price of every commodity to 100 in 2003 and then construct the price index on the basis of the normalized series.

The oil price index is constructed by interacting the oil production value in 2003 with the international oil price ($P_{st}^{oil} = oil_s \times oilpr_t$). We use oil production data published in the Nigerian National Petroleum Corporation (NNPC) Annual Statistical Bulletin. However, because these data are only reported at the oil well level and not at the state level, we had to manually map the oil wells to a state. To do that we use a combination of online google search and geo-mapping using longitudes and latitudes of the oil well mapped to the state.

The oil price index variable should be exogenous to conflict. First, Nigeria is a price taker in the international oil market, as it is a small producer (Nigeria produced approximately 2.8 percent of world oil production in 2012).[14] In addition, oil production at the beginning of the period should not be influenced by subsequent conflict, especially as we control for the level of past conflict (in case there is persistence over time). Given the lack of GDP data by state, we normalize the production by state-wise receipts of Value Added Tax (VAT) in 2003 (Nigeria Bureau of Statistics 2010). The VAT is a tax levied on products and services, based on the contribution to output at each stage of production. Thus low levels of VAT receipts indicate low levels of economic activity, and vice versa. Table A.5 presents the summary statistics for these main regressors along with the other control variables used in the analysis (the statistics for the dependent variable are presented and discussed in appendix B).

The NLSS was designed to collect household characteristics, such as demographic, education, health, and migration, for the purpose of poverty analysis. The survey covered the urban and rural areas of all the 36 states of the Federation and the Federal Capital Territory. Ten Enumeration Areas (EAs) were studied in each of the states every month, while 5 EAs were covered in Abuja. Information on food expenditure and production by 18,770 households was considered.

Part B of the questionnaire asked respondents questions on household's consumption, including both expenditures and agricultural activities at the household level. Household expenditure is categorized into nonfood and food expenses.[15] The former is, in turn, divided into frequently and less frequently purchased items. Table A.4 shows that the mean per capita food expenditure is highest in the South South and South East regions, which house the major oil-producing wells. The South East region had mean total per capita expenditure of N 45,216, which is well above the national average. However, the

Table A.4 Household Per Capita Expenditure on Food and Nonfood by Zone

	Per capita food expenditure	Per capita nonfood expenditure	Total per capita expenditure
South South	17,287	19,199	36,486
South East	22,314	22,902	45,216
South West	16,533	26,696	43,229
North Central	14,740	15,067	29,806
North East	15,364	12,171	27,535
North West	16,907	11,176	28,083
Total	17,094	18,506	35,600

Source: Elaboration on Nigeria Living Standards Survey 2003/04.

Table A.5 Summary Statistics of the Regressors (2004–11)

	Obs.	Mean	SD	Min	Max
CI	296	77.40	23.98	21.92	137.72
PI	296	66.28	26.67	21.19	138.08
CI_{NAR}^{oth}	296	87.44	24.46	45.27	143.69
PI_{NAR}^{oth}	296	75.76	25.62	28.62	127.31
CI_{BR}^{oth}	296	70.55	27.18	23.42	142.07
PI_{BR}^{oth}	296	83.22	25.41	27.30	149.43
CI_{NAR}^{Intl}	296	69.43	21.34	30.18	132.61
PI_{NAR}^{Intl}	296	56.33	13.00	31.43	84.29
Oil index	296	60.27	155.41	0	925.30
President	296	0.28	0.45	0	1
Pop (2003) ln	296	8.15	0.40	7.25	9.15
Pop dens. (2003) ln	296	5.26	0.89	3.93	7.90
Past conflict event	296	29.86	49.31	2	264
Past fatalities	296	202.46	344.81	1	1,892
Past event with fat.	296	17.19	29.59	1	156
Past battle events	296	12.76	21.52	1	99
Past protest	296	5.70	10.20	0	60
Past civil. violence	296	10.84	18.35	0	103
Poverty gap 2003	296	18.46	11.07	5	54
Headcount poverty 2003	296	48.78	17.90	21	87
Multiple dominant groups dummy	296	0.32	0.47	0	1
Ethnic minorities > 2	296	0.68	0.47	0	1

more urban South West region had the highest levels of per capita nonfood expenditures.

The agricultural production section of the survey collects information on agriculture income and assets; land, livestock, and equipment; harvest and disposal of crops; seasonality of sales and purchases (key staples only); and other agricultural income (both in cash and kind). Information on the production of agricultural food is collected at a different frequency. Information on household produce sales during the last 12 months is collected for certain items, such as staple grains, field crops, and cash crops, including the value of sales from hunting, honey, fruit/berries, milk, other dairy products, eggs, hides, wool and skin, and mushrooms output. On the other hand, for roots, fruits, vegetables, and other crops harvested piecemeal, respondents are asked how much the household sold in the last two weeks. We converted these two week estimates to a yearly value of sales.[16]

The West Bank and Gaza

The data in this study were taken from various Palestinian and Israeli sources that include information on the Palestinian labor market, on economic and socio-demographic characteristics of Palestinian localities, on Palestinians fatalities from the conflict, and on Palestinian and Israeli trade. This information was aggregated to the level of the locality, which serves as the unit of analysis and represents the smallest spatial unit for which economic data is available in the West Bank and Gaza. Our sample consists of 532 localities in the West Bank and 37 localities in the Gaza Strip.

Data on the number of Palestinians fatalities from politically motivated violence (Palestinians killed by Israelis) during the Second Intifada (September 2000–December 2004) in each locality are taken from B'Tselem—the Israeli Information Center for Human Rights in the Occupied Territories.[17] B'Tselem publishes detailed data records which include every Israeli and Palestinian fatality during the Second Intifada.

We are also able to identify those Palestinian fatalities which occurred as a result of political demonstrations or confrontation with the Israeli army by examining the description of each fatality provided by B'tselem. As this description is not available for all fatalities, this subset of fatalities is incomplete; so in the subsequent analysis we use it only for robustness purposes.

Locality-level data on Palestinian sectoral employment as well as on socio-demographic characteristics come from the 1997 Palestinian population census carried out by the Palestinian Central Bureau of Statistics (PCBS). The Palestinian census data includes information about various localities' characteristics, such as total population, share of males in the population, share of population between the ages 15–40, share of population with up to elementary education, share of refugees in the population, share of households with more than 8 persons, share of people married in the population, as well as availability of public utilities. Importantly for our purposes, the census also records data on the employment of the population for all private establishments in the PT at the 2-digit ISIC level.

We match this distribution of employment at the locality level with Palestinian and Israeli trade data at the 5-digit SITC level (revision 3) in order to compute the measure of exposure to the trade shocks. Palestinian annual import and export data are taken from the Palestinian Central Bureau of Statistics. Israeli import and export data (at the 5-digit SITC level) come from the COMTRADE dataset in WITS.[18] We also use world and Chinese exports data from the same source.

Other labor market variables were constructed from two sources. Administrative data on all Palestinians employed in Israel with a permit in

1999 come from the Israeli Ministry of Industry Trade and Labor, which is in charge of issuing the permits. In addition we gathered further labor data, including information on Palestinian private and public employment in Israel from the Palestinian Labor Force Survey (PLFS). This survey has been administered every quarter since 1995 to a nationally representative sample of households. We restrict the sample from the PLFS to individuals in the labor force between the ages of 15 and above and surveyed during at least one of the four quarters in 1999. As the survey is not stratified at the locality level, we exclude localities in which less than 30 individuals were interviewed in each round in 1999.[19]

Summary statistics for the key variables at the district level are provided in table A.6.

Table A.6 Summary Statistics for Key Variables in the Israeli-Palestinian Conflict Study

		Obs.	Mean	SD	Min	Max
Palestinian fatalities		569	4.33	21.84	0	331
Localities with at least one fatality		569	0.35	0.48	0	1
Δ Palestinian exports$_{96-99}$		569	3.53	4.36	−6.21	13.48
Δ Palestinian exports to Israel$_{96-99}$		569	4.53	5.48	−5.2	17.16
Δ Israeli imports from RoW$_{96-99}$		569	−11.73	32.78	−144	120.12
Δ Palestinian imports$_{96-99}$		569	25.33	17.61	−4.87	95.18
Δ Palestinian exports to RoW$_{96-99}$		569	−1.00	1.31	−5.29	2.42
Socioeconomic characteristics in 1997 in locality	Total population	569	4,542	18,499	4	353,113
	Share of males in the population	569	0.51	0.03	0.385	1
	Share of population between the ages 15–40	569	0.39	0.04	0.273	0.727
	Share of population with up to elementary education	569	0.61	0.12	0.25	0.973
	Share of refugees in the population	569	0.28	0.32	0	1
	Share of households with more than 8 persons	569	0.34	0.11	0	1
	Share of married in the population	569	0.33	0.03	0.174	0.438
Localities in Gaza Strip		569	0.07	0.25	0	1
Pre-Intifada fatalities		569	0.25	1.44	0	20
Localities in Jerusalem		569	0.05	0.22	0	1
Availability of public utilities in 1997 in locality	Water	569	0.69	0.46	0	1
	Electricity	569	0.84	0.37	0	1
	Sewage	569	0.11	0.31	0	1
	Telephone (landline)	569	0.63	0.48	0	1
Share of employment in Israel in 1999		222	10.63	6.91	0	36.186
Locality type	Urban	222	0.23	0.42	0	1
	Refugee camp	222	0.10	0.30	0	1
Average wage of employees in Israel in 1999		212	100.96	16.08	52.03	150.160
Share of public sector employment in 1999		222	5.65	3.87	0	18.947
Average wage of public sector employees in 1999		209	59.57	35.03	30.66	538.280
Share of private sector employment in 1999		222	9.75	6.81	0.53	41.523
Average wage of private sector employees in 1999		221	61.92	17.35	16.62	150.135

Sources: Authors' elaboration using different datasets; see text for details.
Note: See table A.7 for variables' description.

Table A.7 Description of Variables Used in the Palestinian Case Study

Variable	Description
Palestinian Fatalities	Average number of fatalities from politically motivated violence (Palestinians killed by Israel) from the outbreak of the Second Intifada (September 28, 2000) until December 2004 in the locality. For Palestinian fatalities, the locality is the locality where the fatal wounding occurred. There are a handful of cases in which the fatal wounding occurred inside Israel. In those cases, we considered the locality of residence, or the closest geographical locality.
Localities with at least one fatality	Dummy variable which takes 1 if the locality has more than zero fatalities and 0 if it has 0 fatalities.
Change in the Palestinian exports to Israel between the years 1999 and 1996	Sum of the change in the Palestinian exports to Israel in each sector between the years 1999 and 1996, weighted by the 1997 employment share in that sector in each locality of the total employees in the same locality.
Change in the Israeli imports from the rest of the world between the years 1999 and 1996	Sum of the change in the Israeli imports from the rest of the world (except the West Bank and Gaza) in each sector between the years 1996 and 1999, weighted by the 1997 employment share in that sector in each locality of the total employees in the same locality.
Change in the total Palestinian exports between the years 1996 and 1999	Sum of the change in the total Palestinian exports in each sector between the years 1996 and 1999, weighted by the 1997 employment share in that sector in each locality of the total employees in the same locality.
Change in the total Palestinian imports between the years 1996 and 1999	Sum of the changes in the total Palestinian imports in each sector between the years 1996 and 1999, weighted by the 1997 employment share in that sector in each locality of the total employees in the same locality.
Change in the total Palestinian exports to the rest of the world between the years 1996 and 1999	Sum of the change in the total Palestinian exports from the rest of the world (except Israel) in each sector between the years 1996 and 1999, weighted by the 1997 employment share in that sector in each locality from the total employees in the same locality.
Share of employment in Israel in 1999	Share of Palestinian workers employed in Israel out of total working age in 1999 in the locality.
Average wage of employees in Israel in 1999	Average daily wage of employees in Israel in 1999 in the locality.
Share of public sector employment in 1999	Share of public sector employees out of total working age in 1999 in the locality.
Average wage of public sector employees in 1999	Average daily wage of public sector employees in 1999 in the locality.
Share of private sector employment in 1999	Share of private sector employees out of total working age in 1999 in the locality.
Average wage of private sector employees in 1999	Average daily wage of private sector employees in 1999 in the locality.
Fatalities between January 1995 and August 2000	Average number of fatalities from politically motivated violence (Palestinians killed by Israelis) from 1995 until the outbreak of the Second Intifada (September 28, 2000) in the locality.

Notes

1. These datasets are available at http://www.prio.no/Data/Armed-Conflict /UCDP-PRIO/.

2. For example Bazzi and Blattman (2014) report that in the PRIO dataset major civil wars are coded in 7 percent of the country-years, compared to 20 percent of the country-years in the Fearon and Laitin (2003) data.

3. We first checked the conflict instances that were missing in PRIO according to Gersovitz and Kriger (2013) (i.e. Cameroon, the Central African Republic, the Republic of Congo, Côte d'Ivoire, Kenya–Shifta War [1963–1967], Mali, Niger, and Senegal). All of these conflicts, with the exception of the one in Kenya, have been included in the latest versions of the PRIO dataset while they were still missing in COW. As an additional check, we identified those conflict incidences recorded in COW but missing in the PRIO data (e.g. Liberia in 1996). We find that in various instances, these conflict years had been there in earlier versions of the PRIO data but had been removed in the more recent versions, suggesting a frequent process of updating of the conflict episodes in the PRIO dataset.

4. See the web appendix to Bazzi and Blattman (2014) for the complete list of sources.

5. The list of these commodities is available in a separate web appendix.

6. To avoid the effects of different units of measure across commodities, all international commodity prices are normalized to 100 in 2000.

7. For example, commodity exports could react in anticipation of a conflict or as a reaction to changes in international commodity prices themselves, thus making the contemporaneous export shares invalid as weights.

8. One important concern comes from the fact that some countries are large exporters of these commodities and their internal conditions may influence international prices. We address this issue in the next sections.

9. The index scaled by export-GDP ratio is defined as:

$$Px_{it} = \left(\Pi_j P_{jt}^{exp_{ij,t-k}} \times \left(\frac{\Sigma_j \; exp_{ij,mid\,point}}{GDP_{mid\,point}} \right) \right)^{\frac{1}{\Sigma_j exp_{ij,t-k}}}$$

10. The Living Standard Measurement Survey for Nigeria 2010/11 is not appropriate for the purpose of our analysis for two reasons: the survey is only representative at the geopolitical zone and not at the state level, and the period 2010/11 covers periods after the Niger Delta conflict but before the core of the Boko Haram crisis.

11. Available domestic price data are matched with food and nonfood items in the survey in order to estimate the indices. Items not matched are not used in the indices, but contribute to the weights as described.

12. Though another batch of data is available for 2010–13, there are a number of inconsistencies in the data that make it difficult to use at this point. The NBS changed the methodology of data collection for the prices in those periods and some of the prices were totally different when compared to the 2000–10 dataset. Also the items in the 2010–13 datasets were different with more items included and disaggregated.

13. The broad matching procedure relies on subjective judgments, based on our understanding of the country and the consumption items.

14. http://www.eia.gov/countries/country-data.cfm?fips=NI. Accessed April 29, 2014.

15. The expenditure on food by household is a sum of expenditure on each individual food item over 6 visits. That is, aggregation of the response to the question, "How much was spent on … since my last visit?"

16. One way of converting this is to multiply the two week estimate by 26 to get a total of 52 weeks' value of sale. However, inconsistency in the values reported for cassava,

yam, and plantain, which include data on both two weeks and annual sales, shows that multiplication of the two weeks value by 26 is not a consistent estimate of the yearly value. We therefore elected to predict the yearly value produced by each household, by applying an average of the relationships between the yearly value and the two weeks value reported for cassava, yam, and plantain to the other items.

17. Available at: http://www.btselem.org.

18. This is available at http://wits.worldbank.org/wits/.

19. Given this narrow geographical definition, many localities do not meet this criterion, leaving us with 241 localities. We drop 42 additional localities for which key variables in the analysis are missing.

References

Anderson, K., M. Kurzweil, W. Martin, D. Sandri, and E. Valenzuela. 2008. "Measuring Distortions to Agricultural Incentives, Revisited." Policy Research Working Paper 4612, World Bank.

Arezki, R., and M. Brückner. 2011. "Food Prices, Conflict, and Democratic Change." Mimeo.

Bazzi, S., and C. Blattman. 2014. "Economic Shocks and Conflict: Evidence from Commodity Prices." *American Economic Journal: Macroeconomics*.

Bellows, J., and E. Miguel. 2009. "War and Local Collective Action in Sierra Leone." *Journal of Public Economics* 93 (11–12): 1144–57.

Besley, T., and T. Persson. 2008. "The Incidence of Civil War: Theory and Evidence." Mimeo.

Bruckner, M., and A. Ciccone. 2010. "International Commodity Prices, Growth and the Outbreak of Civil War in Sub-Saharan Africa." *The Economic Journal* 120 (May): 519–34.

Calì, M., and A. Mulabdic. 2014. "Trade and Civil Conflict: Revisiting the Cross-Country Evidence." Policy Research Working Paper, forthcoming.

Deaton, A. 1995. "International Commodity Prices, Macroeconomic Performance, and Politics in Sub-Saharan Africa." Princeton Studies in International Finance, 79, Princeton University.

Fearon, J., and D. Laitin. 2003. "Ethnicity, Insurgency, and Civil War." *American Political Science Review* 97 (1): 75–90.

Gersovitz, M., and N. Kriger. 2013. "What Is a Civil War? A Critical Review of Its Definition and (Econometric) Consequences." *World Bank Research Observer* 28 (2): 159–90.

Hull, P., and M. Imai. 2013. "Economic Shocks and Civil Conflict: Evidence from Foreign Interest Rate Movements." *Journal of Development Economics* 103: 77–89.

Lin, Y-H., and G. Michaels. 2011. "Do Giant Oilfield Discoveries Fuel Internal Armed Conflicts?" CEPR Discussion Paper 8620.

Montalvo, J. G., and M. Reynal-Querol. 2005. "Ethnic Polarization, Potential Conflict, and Civil Wars." *American Economic Review* 95 (3): 796–816.

Nigeria Bureau of Statistics. 2010. Annual Abstract of Statistics.

Nunn, N., and N. Qian. 2014. "U.S. Food Aid and Civil Conflict." *American Economic Review* 104 (6): 1630–66.

Sambanis, N. 2004. "What Is Civil War? Conceptual and Empirical Complexities of an Operational Definition." *Journal of Conflict Resolution* 48: 814–58.

Sarkees, M. R., and F. Wayman. 2010. *Resort to War: 1816–2007*. Washington, DC: CQ Press.

World Bank. 2013. "Harmonized List of Fragile Situations, FY 2014." World Bank, Washington, DC.

———. 2014. World Development Indicators, online dataset.

Estimation Methodology and Empirical Results

Cross-Country Analysis

The main empirical analysis estimates the impact of various trade-related variables on the onset of conflict. We follow Bazzi and Blattman (2014) and model conflict onset and ending separately, using split samples.[1] This strategy allows incorporating the dynamic properties of conflicts (Beck and Katz 2011). These are highly persistent, so past years of conflicts affect current conflict. As the former are in turn affected by past shocks, not modeling the dynamics introduces a bias in the estimation. The basic specification reads as follows:

$$CO_{it} = \alpha_i + \sum_{j=0}^{n} \beta_j Px_{it-j} + \sum_{j=0}^{n} \gamma_j Pm_{it-j}$$
$$+ \sum_{j=0}^{n} \theta_j MP_{it-j} + \vartheta TN_{it-1} + \Gamma X_{it} + \rho_t + \varepsilon_{it} \qquad (B.1)$$

$$CE_{it} = \alpha_i + \sum_{j=0}^{n} \beta_j Px_{it-j} + \sum_{j=0}^{n} \gamma_j Pm_{it-j}$$
$$+ \sum_{j=0}^{n} \theta_j MP_{it-j} + \vartheta TN_{it-1} + \Gamma X_{it} + \rho_t + \varepsilon_{it} \qquad (B.2)$$

where CO and CE are conflict onset and ending (as defined above) for country I at time t, Px is the (country-specific) export price index, Pm is the import price index; MP is a country-specific market potential variable; TN is the share of i's trade with its neighbors (i.e. countries with which it shares a border) in total trade; X is a vector of time varying controls, α are country fixed effects, ρ are time effects, and ε is the i.i.d. error term. The errors are corrected for clustering at the country level. The use of country fixed effects controls for any time invariant factors that may influence the probability of conflict, such as geography, ethnicity, religion, and colonial history. In addition, the different lags in the price regressor account for the time-dependence of these shocks, which are usually negatively autocorrelated and can take many periods to affect earnings.[2]

Unlike the other trade variables, TN does not have a lag structure, since it is highly persistent and one single lag appears appropriate to capture its effect on conflict while reducing the potential endogeneity concerns. We argue that the other three trade variables—*Px*, *Pm*, and *MP*—are also exogenous to the individual countries' conditions that are associated with the probability of conflict. These variables capture the variation in demand and supply in international goods markets and in a country's trading partners. These factors should not be influenced significantly by conditions in individual countries.

An exception to this rule is when the countries are large enough to influence the international supply and/or demand in certain markets. If world prices rise in anticipation of conflict, this may lead to a spurious positive correlation between conflict and the lagged price index. In our sample there are 16 cases of a country producing on average more than 20 percent of global exports of a particular commodity. One way to deal with this issue is to exclude the commodity in question from the country's price index, which is what Bazzi and Blattman (2014) do. However, that may introduce another source of bias. Consider for instance coffee production in Colombia. The country is responsible for 14 percent of global coffee exports. Dube and Vargas (2013) show that the sharp fall in international coffee prices in the 1990s substantially increased conflict intensity in Colombia. Thus excluding coffee from Colombia's price index would bias the *Px* coefficient upward. Because of this reason we do not exclude any commodities from the price variables in the baseline specifications. Instead, we check the robustness of the results to the exclusion of relevant commodities (according to different thresholds) as well as of some countries that are price makers in at least one commodity (average share in global exports above the threshold).

The vector X contains controls that are likely to have an independent effect on conflict. First, we include a dummy for whether the country has had any conflict since World War II, which captures the higher likelihood of starting a conflict for countries which already experienced one recently (World Bank 2011). Second, in order to control for the spillover effects of conflict, we include a dummy for whether any of the neighboring countries has a civil conflict. The variable is lagged one year to reduce the endogeneity concerns. In some specifications we also include the incidence of coup attempts (whether successful or not) in the two years prior to *t*, based on Powell and Thyne (2011). This can be interpreted as an indicator of a weak state (Kuhn and Weidmann 2013), but it could also act as a trigger for a civil conflict itself.

To differentiate the effects across classes of commodities (see chapter 1), we split the Px variables into different groups of commodities. In particular, we distinguish between point-source and diffused commodities as well as between commodities that are consumed in the country and those that are not. This yields four different export price variables, each with a lag structure.

We use the linear probability model as in Bazzi and Blattman (2014) to estimate equations (B.1) and (B.2), although the results are very similar when using the conditional fixed effect logit and the probit estimator as well (results available upon request).

One problem with estimating equations (B.1) and (B.2) is that the dependent variables have a very large number of zeros relative to the number of ones, i.e. the models try to explain rare events.[3] That is inherent in the nature of this type of empirical analysis, although it is rarely acknowledged in other studies. Importantly, this problem can lead to biased coefficients' estimates in finite samples (King and Zeng 2001). In addition, the bias in the standard errors tends to go in the same direction as the bias in the coefficients. Thus the rare event bias may cause the underestimation of event probabilities. King and Zeng (2001) suggest that one way to correct the problem is to decrease the rareness of the event. That could be done, for example, by lowering the threshold of what constitutes an event or by expanding the data selection period. In our case this would strengthen the case for using *any civil conflict* as the dependent variable. For this variable the number of events is 25 times smaller than the number of zeros while it is 50 times smaller for *major conflict onset*. We explore in more detail in the main text the implications of this possible bias in interpreting the empirical results.[4]

While the main focus of the analysis is to identify the effects of the trade variables on conflict onset (and ending), we also examine their impact on the intensity of conflicts. This is an important outcome in its own right and may not necessarily follow the same dynamics of conflict onset. To that end we also run the following specification:

$$BD_{it} = \alpha_i + \sum_{j=0}^{n} \beta_j Px_{it-j} + \sum_{j=0}^{n} \gamma_j Pm_{it-j}$$
$$+ \sum_{j=0}^{n} \theta_j MP_{it-j} + \vartheta TN_{it-1} + \Gamma X_{it} + t + \varepsilon_{it} \qquad (B.3)$$

where BD is the number of battle-related deaths in country i at time t. The vector X includes also a dummy for the first year of conflict to capture the impact of conflict onset on the intensity of conflict (relative to both the years without conflict and the years with conflict after the first). The vector X also includes a variable measuring the number of years of conflict since the onset.

As we estimate the model over the entire sample (including nonconflict years) this specification combines the effects on the extensive margin (the probability of conflict) with those on the intensive margin (conflict intensity once the conflict has started). This specification is different to that used in Bazzi and Blattman (2014), who run it only on conflict years. We argue that it is important to keep the nonconflict years as well, to capture the effect of the trade variables on a continuum of conflict intensity which varies from none to severe conflict. This specification is similar to that used in most micro studies on the determinants of conflict (e.g. Dube and Vargas 2013). This specification also allows us to avoid the contentious issue of defining the correct threshold for a civil conflict (Chaudion, Peskowitz, and Stanton 2012).

A number of options are available to estimate equation (B.3) in a way that accounts for the fact that the dependent variable is a count variable with a large proportion of zeros, i.e. the poisson, negative binomial or zero-inflated negative binomial estimator (ZINB). In our setup the ZINB estimator is ruled out due to a lack of convergence. As in our dependent variables the unconditional variance is larger than the mean, the negative binomial is to be preferred to the poisson estimator (Long and Freese 2006; Cameron and Trivedi 2013).

Table B.1 The Impact of Trade on Conflict, Cross-Country Analysis

	(1)	(2)	(3)	(4)	(5)	(6)	(7)	(8)
	Any onset	Any onset	Any onset	Any onset	Major onset	Major onset	Major onset	Major onset
Px (t)	0.040**	0.039**	0.039**	0.010*	0.012	0.008	0.008	0.003
	(0.016)	(0.016)	(0.016)	(0.005)	(0.011)	(0.011)	(0.011)	(0.004)
Px (t−1)	−0.014	−0.014	−0.015	0.003	−0.020**	−0.016*	−0.016*	−0.003
	(0.020)	(0.020)	(0.020)	(0.006)	(0.009)	(0.009)	(0.009)	(0.003)
Px (t−2)	0.000	0.001	0.001	−0.005	0.007	0.005	0.005	−0.003
	(0.017)	(0.017)	(0.017)	(0.005)	(0.009)	(0.008)	(0.008)	(0.003)
Pm (t)		−0.001	−0.001	0.002		−0.022	−0.022	−0.005
		(0.024)	(0.024)	(0.006)		(0.014)	(0.014)	(0.004)
Pm (t−1)		−0.002	−0.003	0.003		0.017	0.017	0.000
		(0.026)	(0.026)	(0.007)		(0.016)	(0.016)	(0.004)
Pm (t−2)		−0.009	−0.009	−0.001		−0.001	−0.001	0.002
		(0.023)	(0.022)	(0.006)		(0.014)	(0.014)	(0.003)
MP (t)		−0.006	−0.006	−0.001		0.005	0.005	0.000
		(0.023)	(0.023)	(0.004)		(0.010)	(0.010)	(0.002)
MP (t−1)		−0.041	−0.042	−0.008		−0.038	−0.038	−0.005
		(0.054)	(0.054)	(0.010)		(0.036)	(0.036)	(0.007)
MP (t−2)		0.061	0.063	0.007		0.052	0.052	0.006
		(0.066)	(0.065)	(0.012)		(0.047)	(0.047)	(0.011)
Trade with neigh. (t−1)		−0.033	−0.031	−0.037		−0.018	−0.018	−0.018
		(0.053)	(0.054)	(0.057)		(0.032)	(0.032)	(0.035)
Any conflict since 1946	0.179***	0.183***	0.185***	0.177***	0.046***	0.045***	0.045***	0.047***
	(0.021)	(0.021)	(0.021)	(0.021)	(0.012)	(0.012)	(0.012)	(0.012)
War border (t−1)		−0.006	−0.007	−0.007		0.002	0.002	0.003
		(0.012)	(0.012)	(0.012)		(0.008)	(0.008)	(0.008)
Coup			−0.018	−0.015			−0.001	−0.001
			(0.016)	(0.018)			(0.008)	(0.008)
Observations	3,465	3,428	3,428	3,327	3,861	3,812	3,812	3,704
R-sq. (within)	0.069	0.072	0.072	0.068	0.025	0.026	0.026	0.026
Countries	114	114	114	114	115	115	115	115
Shocks	logP	logP	logP	Δlogp	logP	logP	logP	Δlogp
Weight	[t−12;t−2]	[t−12;t−2]	[t−12;t−2]	[t−12;t−2]	[t−12;t−2]	[t−12;t−2]	[t−12;t−2]	[t−12;t−2]
Time trends	NO	NO	NO	NO	NO	NO	NO	NO
Sum Px	0.026**	0.026**	0.025**	0.008	−0.001	−0.002	−0.002	−0.002
Sum Pm		−0.013	−0.013	0.004		−0.006	−0.006	−0.003
Sum MP		0.015	0.016	−0.002		0.019	0.019	0.001

Note: Robust standard errors (clustered at the country level) in parentheses.
*** $p < 0.01$, ** $p < 0.05$, * $p < 0.1$.

Table B.2 Robustness with Fast-Moving, Country-Specific Time Trends, Cross-Country Analysis

	(1)	(2)	(3)	(4)	(5)	(6)
	Any onset	Any onset	Any onset	Major onset	Major onset	Major onset
Px (t)	0.037**	0.035**	0.033**	0.010	0.006	0.007
	(0.017)	(0.015)	(0.016)	(0.011)	(0.010)	(0.010)
Px (t−1)	−0.015	−0.016	−0.015	−0.015*	−0.015*	−0.014*
	(0.020)	(0.020)	(0.020)	(0.009)	(0.008)	(0.008)
Px (t−2)	0.008	0.003	0.008	0.008	0.006	0.009
	(0.019)	(0.017)	(0.018)	(0.009)	(0.007)	(0.008)
Pm (t)	0.007	0.011	0.017	−0.021	−0.005	−0.003
	(0.026)	(0.023)	(0.025)	(0.015)	(0.011)	(0.012)
Pm (t−1)	−0.007	−0.021	−0.023	0.015	0.003	0.004
	(0.026)	(0.022)	(0.022)	(0.016)	(0.014)	(0.014)
Pm (t−2)	0.001	0.001	0.010	0.004	0.001	0.004
	(0.025)	(0.017)	(0.020)	(0.016)	(0.010)	(0.011)
MP (t)	−0.015	−0.016	−0.027	−0.007	−0.009	−0.024**
	(0.023)	(0.022)	(0.024)	(0.011)	(0.011)	(0.012)
MP (t−1)	−0.043	−0.031	−0.052	−0.038	−0.026	−0.031
	(0.055)	(0.048)	(0.050)	(0.038)	(0.038)	(0.042)
MP (t−2)	0.068	0.057	0.093	0.059	0.053	0.068
	(0.070)	(0.057)	(0.066)	(0.051)	(0.054)	(0.060)
Trade with neigh.	−0.084	−0.030	−0.080	−0.038	−0.015	−0.036
(t−1)	(0.059)	(0.054)	(0.057)	(0.041)	(0.033)	(0.041)
Controls	YES	YES	YES	YES	YES	YES
Observations	3,428	3,425	3,425	3,812	3,809	3,809
R–sq. (within)	0.156	0.072	0.157	0.064	0.027	0.066
Countries	114	114	114	115	115	115
Shocks	logP	logP	logP	logP	logP	logP
Weight	[t−12; t−2]	[t−4; t−2]	[t−4; t−2]	[t−12; t−2]	[t−4; t−2]	[t−4; t−2]
Time trends	YES	NO	YES	YES	NO	YES
Sum Px	0.030*	0.022**	0.025	0.003	−0.003	0.002
Sum Pm	−0.00003	−0.009	0.003	−0.002	−0.002	0.005
Sum MP	0.010	0.010	0.014	0.013	0.018	0.013

Note: Robust standard errors (clustered at the country level) in parentheses; controls include any conflict since 1946 and war border (t−1).
***p < 0.01, **p < 0.05, *p < 0.1.

Table B.3 Robustness for Price Makers and Conflict Data Source, Cross-Country Analysis

	(1)	(2)	(3)	(4)	(5)	(6)
Conflict data	PRIO	PRIO	PRIO	PRIO	PRIO	COW
Dep. Var.	Any onset	Any onset	Any onset	Any onset	Major (1,000)	Major (1,000)
Px (t)	0.028*	0.040**	0.040**	0.043**	0.006	0.018**
	(0.016)	(0.018)	(0.016)	(0.016)	(0.010)	(0.009)
Px (t−1)	−0.012	−0.023	−0.022	−0.025	−0.019*	−0.025**
	(0.020)	(0.022)	(0.020)	(0.021)	(0.011)	(0.011)
Px (t−2)	0.001	0.007	0.005	0.008	0.004	0.011
	(0.017)	(0.019)	(0.017)	(0.017)	(0.008)	(0.009)
Pm (t)	−0.006	0.002	−0.001	0.009	−0.007	0.037**
	(0.024)	(0.027)	(0.024)	(0.025)	(0.017)	(0.017)
Pm (t−1)	−0.001	−0.006	−0.004	−0.009	0.005	−0.017
	(0.026)	(0.031)	(0.026)	(0.028)	(0.017)	(0.021)

table continues next page

Table B.3 Robustness for Price Makers and Conflict Data Source, Cross-Country Analysis *(continued)*

	(1)	(2)	(3)	(4)	(5)	(6)
Conflict data	PRIO	PRIO	PRIO	PRIO	PRIO	COW
Dep. Var.	Any onset	Any onset	Any onset	Any onset	Major (1,000)	Major (1,000)
Pm (t−2)	−0.008	−0.017	−0.008	−0.013	−0.008	−0.007
	(0.022)	(0.027)	(0.022)	(0.024)	(0.015)	(0.014)
MP (t)	−0.004	0.001	−0.007	−0.001	0.005	0.001
	(0.023)	(0.024)	(0.023)	(0.023)	(0.012)	(0.009)
MP (t−1)	−0.042	−0.062	−0.038	−0.035	−0.032	−0.030
	(0.054)	(0.059)	(0.054)	(0.056)	(0.046)	(0.043)
MP (t−2)	0.061	0.081	0.059	0.049	0.043	0.057
	(0.065)	(0.070)	(0.066)	(0.067)	(0.057)	(0.061)
Trade with neigh.	−0.034	−0.053	−0.033	−0.025	−0.037	0.003
(t−1)	(0.053)	(0.055)	(0.053)	(0.053)	(0.034)	(0.036)
Observations	3,428	2,491	3,428	2,992	4,001	3,834
R-sq. (within)	0.070	0.084	0.071	0.079	0.024	0.036
Countries	114	85	114	98	115	115
Threshold	10%	10%	20%	20%	None	None
Exclude	Commod.	Countries	Commod.	Countries	None	None
Sum Px	0.017*	0.024**	0.023**	0.025**	−0.009	0.004
Sum Pm	−0.015	−0.022	−0.014	−0.013	−0.010	0.013
Sum MP	0.015	0.020	0.015	0.013	0.016	0.028

Note: Robust standard errors (clustered at the country level) in parentheses; all regressions include country fixed effects, year effects and controls (any conflict since 1946 and war border (t−1)); trade shock variables are weighted using the slow-moving averages (without country-specific time trends).
***$p < 0.01$, **$p < 0.05$, *$p < 0.1$.

Table B.4 Splitting the Commodities' Variables into Different Types, Cross-Country Analysis

	(1)	(2)	(3)
	onset_any	onset_any	onset_any
Sum Px point-source	0.018*		
	(0.01)		
Sum Px diffused	0.013		
	(0.013)		
Sum Px consumed		0.017*	
		(0.009)	
Sum Px not consumed		0.022	
		(0.017)	
Sum Px point-source consumed			0.032
			(0.033)
Sum Px point-source not consumed			0.013
			(0.015)
Sum Px diffused consumed			−0.019
			(0.015)
Sum Px diffused not consumed			0.021
			(0.015)
Other trade variables	YES	YES	YES
Controls	YES	YES	YES
Weight	[t−12; t−2]	[t−12; t−2]	[t−12; t−2]
Observations	3,403	3,426	3,104
R-sq. (within)	0.070	0.072	0.072
Countries	114	114	114

Note: Robust standard errors (clustered at the country level) in parentheses; all regressions include country fixed effects, year effects and controls (any conflict since 1946 and war border (t−1)); other trade variables include MP and Pm with their three lags and trade with neighbors (t−1).
***$p < 0.01$, **$p < 0.05$, *$p < 0.1$.

Table B.5 The Impact of Trade Variables on the Likelihood of Conflict Coming to an End, Cross-Country Analysis

	(1)	(2)	(3)	(4)	(5)	(6)	(7)	(8)
	Any ending	Any ending	Any ending	Any ending	Major ending	Major ending	Major ending	Major ending
Px (t)	-0.047	-0.053	-0.037	-0.038	0.019	0.020	0.038	0.061
	(0.036)	(0.034)	(0.033)	(0.030)	(0.059)	(0.077)	(0.041)	(0.057)
Px (t−1)	0.040	0.033	0.036	0.028	-0.004	-0.013	-0.045	-0.056
	(0.054)	(0.055)	(0.052)	(0.052)	(0.065)	(0.059)	(0.061)	(0.055)
Px (t−2)	-0.002	-0.024	-0.011	-0.043	0.009	0.034	0.014	0.030
	(0.036)	(0.036)	(0.037)	(0.036)	(0.053)	(0.058)	(0.050)	(0.057)
Pm (t)	-0.044	-0.046	-0.033	-0.042	0.242*	0.237*	0.094	0.179*
	(0.070)	(0.080)	(0.059)	(0.063)	(0.127)	(0.140)	(0.088)	(0.105)
Pm (t−1)	0.129	0.098	0.101	0.077	-0.142	-0.143	-0.131	-0.142
	(0.102)	(0.101)	(0.083)	(0.079)	(0.169)	(0.159)	(0.127)	(0.119)
Pm (t−2)	0.020	0.007	0.021	0.002	0.075	0.082	0.101	0.044
	(0.080)	(0.089)	(0.071)	(0.078)	(0.134)	(0.167)	(0.098)	(0.098)
MP (t)	-0.093	-0.078	-0.050	-0.030	0.123	0.181	0.357	0.399
	(0.180)	(0.191)	(0.148)	(0.172)	(0.347)	(0.343)	(0.252)	(0.305)
MP (t−1)	0.060	-0.064	0.187	0.094	0.114	-0.084	-0.379	-0.571
	(0.332)	(0.312)	(0.268)	(0.258)	(0.479)	(0.432)	(0.409)	(0.394)
MP (t−2)	-0.079	-0.018	-0.278	-0.249	-0.320	0.032	-0.038	0.229
	(0.293)	(0.334)	(0.234)	(0.260)	(0.426)	(0.604)	(0.331)	(0.412)
Trade with neigh. (t−1)	0.249**	0.199*	0.221**	0.155	0.402	0.463	0.359	0.375
	(0.095)	(0.116)	(0.094)	(0.108)	(0.276)	(0.436)	(0.268)	(0.415)
Observations	1,104	1,104	1,101	1,101	540	540	537	537
R-sq. (within)	0.058	0.196	0.056	0.196	0.168	0.297	0.168	0.303
Countries	80	80	80	80	41	41	41	41
Shocks	logP	logP	logP	logP	logP	logP	logP	logP
Weight	[t-12;t-2]	[t-12;t-2]	[t-4;t-2]	[t-4;t-2]	[t-12;t-2]	[t-12;t-2]	[t-4;t-2]	[t-4;t-2]
Time trends	NO	YES	NO	YES	NO	YES	NO	YES
Sum Px	-0.008	-0.045	-0.011	-0.053	0.024	0.041	0.007	0.035
Sum Pm	0.105***	0.058	0.089**	0.037	0.174**	0.177	0.064	0.081
Sum MP	-0.113	-0.16	-0.141	-0.185	-0.082	0.129	-0.059	0.056

Note: Robust standard errors (clustered at the country level) in parentheses; all regressions include country fixed effects, year effects and controls (any conflict since 1946 and war border (t−1)).

***p < 0.01, **p < 0.05, *p < 0.1.

Table B.6 The Impact of Trade on Battle Deaths, Cross-Country Analysis

	(1)	(2)	(3)	(4)
	Battle deaths	Battle deaths	Battle deaths	Battle deaths
Sum Px	0.202***		0.169***	
	(0.053)		(0.052)	
Sum Pm	0.217***	0.278***	0.276***	0.326***
	(0.073)	(0.088)	(0.074)	(0.088)
Sum MP	−0.55***	−0.534***	−0.486***	−0.543***
	(0.168)	(0.172)	(0.162)	(0.169)
Trade with neigh. (t−1)	−2.119***	−1.972***	−2.097***	−1.939***
	(0.284)	(0.289)	(0.285)	(0.295)
Sum Px point-source		−0.038		0.011 (0.069)
		(0.066)		
Sum Px diffused		0.130**		0.062 (0.057)
		(0.057)		
Sum Px consumed				
Sum Px not consumed				
First year	1.704***	1.690***	1.699***	1.679***
	(0.088)	(0.087)	(0.088)	(0.089)
Duration	0.106***	0.106***	0.106***	0.105***
	(0.004)	(0.004)	(0.004)	(0.005)
Controls	YES	YES	YES	YES
Weights	[t−12; t−2]	[t−12; t−2]	[t−4; t−2]	[t−4; t−2]
Observations	3,125	3,110	3,121	3,051
Countries	76	76	76	76

Note: Robust standard errors (clustered at the country level) in parentheses; models are estimated through the negative binomial estimator; all regressions include country fixed effects, a time trend and other controls (any conflict since 1946 and war border (t−1)); trade shock variables are weighted using the slow-moving averages (no country-specific time trends).

***$p < 0.01$, **$p < 0.05$, *$p < 0.1$.

Table B.7 The Effect of Trading with Neighbors on Conflict, Revisited, Cross-Country Analysis

	(1)	(2)	(3)	(4)	(5)	(6)	(7)	(8)
	Any onset	Any onset	Any onset	Any onset	Major onset	Major onset	Major onset	Major onset
Trade with neighbors$_{(RTA)}$ (t−1)	−0.077**	−0.106	−0.084**	−0.113*	0.000	−0.006	−0.005	−0.008
	(0.040)	(0.065)	(0.040)	(0.064)	(0.021)	(0.025)	(0.022)	(0.026)
Instrumented	NO	NO	NO	NO	YES	YES	YES	YES
Time trends	NO	YES	NO	YES	NO	YES	NO	YES
Weights	[t−12; t−2]	[t−12; t−2]	[t−4; t−2]	[t−4; t−2]	[t−12; t−2]	[t−12; t−2]	[t−4; t−2]	[t−4; t−2]
Observations	3,464	3,464	3,461	3,461	3,461	3,461	3,461	3,461
R-squared	0.071	0.158	0.071	0.158	0.071	0.158	0.071	0.158
Nr. of countries	114	114	114	114	114	114	114	114
First stage Kleibergen-Paap								

	(9)	(10)	(11)	(12)	(13)	(14)	(15)	(16)
Trade with neighbors$_{(RTA)}$ (t−1)	−0.077**	−0.108*	−0.077***	−0.108*	−0.007	−0.015	−0.007	−0.015
	(0.038)	(0.055)	(0.038)	(0.055)	(0.018)	(0.021)	(0.018)	(0.021)
Instrumented	NO	NO	NO	NO	YES	YES	YES	YES
Time trends	NO	YES	NO	YES	NO	YES	NO	YES
Weights	[t−12; t−2]	[t−12; t−2]	[t−4; t−2]	[t−4; t−2]	[t−12; t−2]	[t−12; t−2]	[t−4; t−2]	[t−4; t−2]
Observations	3,860	3,860	3,857	3,857	3,857	3,857	3,857	3,857
R-squared	0.026	0.067	0.026	0.065	0.026	0.065	0.026	0.065
Number of countries	115	115	115	115	115	115	115	115
First stage Kleibergen-Paap	22,743	6,948	2,2743	6,948	27,094	8,503	27,094	8,503

Note: Robust standard errors (clustered at the country level) in parentheses; all regressions include country fixed effects, year effects and the trade shocks variables as in the previous tables and other controls (any conflict since 1946 and war border (t−1)); trade shock variables are weighted using the slow-moving averages (no country-specific time trends).

*** $p < 0.01$, ** $p < 0.05$, * $p < 0.1$.

Table B.8 Trade Variables without Lag Structure, Cross-Country Analysis

	(1)	(2)	(3)	(4)
	Any onset	Any onset	Major onset	Major onset
Px (t)	0.029***	0.028*	−0.000	0.005
	(0.010)	(0.015)	(0.005)	(0.009)
Pm (t)	−0.005	0.003	−0.007	−0.003
	(0.016)	(0.022)	(0.008)	(0.010)
MP (t)	−0.001	−0.021	0.003	−0.003
	(0.012)	(0.018)	(0.004)	(0.008)
Trade with neigh. (t − 1)	−0.017	−0.060	−0.014	−0.030
	(0.048)	(0.056)	(0.029)	(0.036)
Controls	YES	YES	YES	YES
Observations	3,628	3,628	4,017	4,017
R-sq. (within)	0.074	0.152	0.025	0.059
Countries	115	115	115	115
Shocks	YES	YES	YES	YES
Time trends	logP	logP	logP	logP

Note: Robust standard errors (clustered at the country level) in parentheses; all regressions include country fixed effects, year effects and controls (any conflict since 1946 and war border (t-1)); trade shock variables are weighted using the slow-moving averages.
***$p < 0.01$, **$p < 0.05$, *$p < 0.1$.

Nigeria

We use the indices developed in appendix A in the regression framework to measuring the impact of price shocks on conflict. The basic specification reads as follows:

$$C_{srt} = \alpha_{rt} + \beta_1 CI_{st-1} + \beta_2 PI_{st-1} + \beta_3 P_{st-1}^{oil}$$
$$+ \beta_4 P_{st-1}^{oil} \times d_{2009} + AZ_s + BX_{st} + \varepsilon_{st}$$

(B.4)

where C is a measure of conflict (e.g. number of conflict episodes, number of violent episodes, number of conflict-related fatalities), P^{oil} is the oil price index, d_{2009} is a post-2009 dummy which captures the period after the amnesty deal between the state and the militant groups in the Niger Delta; Z and X are vectors of time invariant and time varying state-level covariates of conflict, respectively, α are region-time fixed effects, which capture any time varying effect at the regional level. The standard errors are clustered at the state level.

The count nature of the data on conflict makes applying an ordinary linear regression model problematic. The Poisson and Negative Binomial models are the two commonly used models for this kind of data characteristics (count data), because they ensure a positive conditional mean of the conflict variables. The Poisson model has the advantage that it does not require that the model be Poisson distributed to use it—that is, the model requires a weaker distributional

Table B.9 Summary Statistics of the Dependent Variable (2004–11), Nigeria

Variable	Obs	Mean	Std. Dev.	Min	Max	% of Zeroes
Nr. of fatalities from conflict episodes	296	18.4	85.5	0	1,001	41.6
Nr. of conflict events in a year	296	6.9	12.7	0	118	21.3
Number of conflict events with fatalities	296	2.2	6.0	0	79	41.6

Source: ACLED.

assumption than the negative binomial model. However, the negative binomial model is designed to handle over-dispersion in the data and will lead to higher efficiency in estimation.[5] The summary statistics of the main dependent variables (reported in table B.9) confirm that the data is over-dispersed with standard deviations much larger than the mean. Thus we opt to use the negative binomial over the poisson estimator.

Among the controls, Z includes a number of important variables measured at the beginning of the period of analysis (from the NSS), i.e. population, population density, and measures of poverty and inequality, including the headcount poverty rate, poverty gap, and the Gini index of inequality. Z also includes the cost of travelling to Lagos (Nigeria's main trading center), the number of conflict events between 1997 and 2003, and ethnic variables. Ideally we would use measures of ethnic divisions traditionally used in the conflict literature, such as ethnic fractionalization (Alesina et al. 2003) and polarization (Montalvo and Reynal-Querol 2005). However, in the absence of state-level data on the ethnic composition of the population, the next best variable we can construct is a dummy for whether there are more than two ethnic minorities in the state.[6]

We also construct two time-varying ethnic measures of the relation between the state's dominant ethnic group(s) and the ethnic group holding the presidency, which are included in X. The first (*president*) equals 1 if the ethnicity of the nation's president is the same as that of one of the state's dominant groups. This variable captures the idea that federal policies toward the states may be driven, in part, by ethnic allegiance. The second is a dummy variable for those states in which the president variable equals 1 and which have only one dominant ethnic group. This allows us to differentiate the *president*'s effect between these two types of states.

This wide range of state-level covariates, along with region effects, should compensate for the absence of state fixed effects in the regressions.

We propose four sets of indices—two for the consumption and two for the production indices—as instruments to check the endogeneity of price indices to conflict. These indices are constructed in the same way as *CI* and *PI* (see appendix A), but using prices which are arguably exogenous to the conflict at the state level. The first set of price indices is the standard one based on international prices that the literature usually employs as a direct regressor in the absence of domestic price data (e.g. Bazzi and Blattman 2014; Dube and Vargas 2013). The instrument is constructed as follows:

$$C_{st}^{Intl} = \left[\Pi_{j=1}^{I} \left(p_{jt}^{Intl} \right)^{Expshr_{sj}^{2003}} \right] \times \frac{\Sigma_{j=1}^{I} Exptot_{sj}^{2003}}{TotExp_{s}^{2003}} \tag{B.5}$$

where P_{jt}^{Intl} is the international price of good j at time t. This approach has several difficulties. Replacing domestic with international prices requires changing the set of goods included in the index. The range of goods for which international prices are available (from 1 to I) is more limited than the N or K goods included in equations (A.5) and (A.6) of the section on Nigeria of appendix A. International prices are available only for internationally traded commodities, which often do not include many local products important for consumption and production in Nigeria (e.g. yam and cassava). The amount of survey data matched to international prices is more limited than the amount matched with domestic prices, i.e. the scaling term for these instruments is smaller than in the CI and PI in equations (A.5) and (A.6) of appendix A. The same applies to the PI instrument as well. Moreover, international prices do not account for the price transmission from international to domestic markets, which is often limited. Thus international prices may not provide an ideal representation of the size of the price shock at the local level.

We propose another set of instruments to address both issues. The instruments are constructed using domestic prices of faraway states, following the same logic of Jacoby (2013) for changes in rice prices in Indian districts. The price data for the other Nigerian states should reflect exogenous international price changes, their transmission to the domestic market, and shifts in demand and supply in the large domestic market outside of the particular state. We exclude neighboring states that may be affected by the conditions in the state in question, to ensure the exogeneity of the instruments.[7]

For each state s, we compute the weighted average of prices of states located beyond a certain travel distance (D) to the capital of state s—weighted by the inverse of D:

$$p_{jst}^{other} = \Sigma_{m=1}^{N_S} \frac{1}{D_m} \times p_{jmt} \tag{B.6}$$

where p_{jmt} is the price of j in state m at time t for all the N_s states whose capital is located beyond 11 hours travel distance. The eleven hours threshold is based on both the mean and median bilateral distance between the state capitals. We argue that this threshold excludes all the states that are close to the state's geopolitical zone of influence. On average, about 10 states are included on the basis of this threshold. Differently from Jacoby (2013), we penalize far-away state's prices, conditional on being more than 11 hours away, by applying the inverse distance weight. This ensures that within the set of states beyond 11 hours, those relatively closer to the state in question have a greater weight.[8]

We then replace the p_{jst} in equation (A.5) of appendix A with p_{jst}^{other} to obtain the instrument CI_{st}^{oth}. We also do the same for PI. Note that the rest of equation (B.5) is unchanged, as the goods j are the same in equations (A.5) and (A.6) in appendix A, since the price data come from the same source (Nigeria Bureau of Statistics). That is, of course, the case for both the narrow and the broad matching of goods between the price and the survey data. It is also the case for the production indices defined in equation (A.6) of appendix A.

Following Cameron and Trivedi (2013), we use these instruments to extract the endogenous component of CI and PI through the first stage regressions. We use the instruments in separate regressions:

$$CI_{srt} = \alpha_{rt} + \delta_1^{oth} CI_{st}^{oth} + \delta_2^{oth} PI_{st}^{oth} + \delta_3 P_{st}^{oil} + \delta_4 P_{st}^{oil} \times d_{2009} + Z_s + X_{st} + \mu_{st} \qquad \text{(B.7)}$$

$$PI_{srt} = \alpha_{rt} + \delta_1^{intl} CI_{st}^{oth} + \delta_2^{intl} PI_{st}^{oth} + \delta_3 P_{st}^{oil} + \delta_4 P_{st}^{oil} \times d_{2009} + Z_s + X_{st} + v_{st} \qquad \text{(B.8)}$$

$$CI_{srt} = \alpha_{rt} + \delta_1 CI_{st}^{intl} + \delta_2 PI_{st}^{intl} + \delta_3 P_{st}^{oil} + \delta_4 P_{st}^{oil} \times d_{2009} + Z_s + X_{st} + \mu_{st} \qquad \text{(B.7')}$$

$$PI_{srt} = \alpha_{rt} + \delta_1 CI_{st}^{intl} + \delta_2 PI_{st}^{intl} + \delta_3 P_{st}^{oil} + \delta_4 P_{st}^{oil} \times d_{2009} + Z_s + X_{st} + v_{st} \qquad \text{(B.8')}$$

Table B.10 The Impact of Price Shocks on Conflict Events in Nigeria (2004–11)

	(1)	(2)	(3)	(4)	(5)	(6)
Dep. Variable	Any event	Any event	Any event	Any event	Any event	Any event
Instruments	PI_{NAR}^{oth}	PI_{NAR}^{oth}	$CI_{NAR}^{oth}, PI_{NAF}^{oth}$	$CI_{BR}^{oth}, PI_{BR}^{oth}$	$CI_{NAR}^{Intl}, PI_{NAR}^{Intl}$	$CI_{BR}^{Intl}, PI_{BR}^{Intl}$
$CI_{NAR}(t-1)$			0.052***		0.053*	
			(0.013)		(0.030)	
$PI_{NAR}(t-1)$	0.054	0.024	−0.047***		−0.001	
	(0.053)	(0.052)	(0.012)		(0.025)	
Oil ind. (t−1)		0.002**	0.003***	0.003***	0.003***	0.003***
		(0.001)	(0.001)	(0.001)	(0.001)	(0.001)
Oil ind. (t−1) x post-09		−0.003***	−0.003***	−0.003***	−0.003***	−0.003***
		(0.001)	(0.001)	(0.001)	(0.001)	(0.001)
$CI_{BR}(t-1)$				0.038***		0.078*
				(0.011)		(0.043)
$PI_{BR}(t-1)$				−0.036***		−0.008
				(0.01)		(0.026)
Marginal effects: change in number of conflict events caused by a 10% increase in price index						
CI			2.97	2.31	2.83	4.51
PI		−	−2.30	−1.86	−0.05	−0.39
Oil ind.		0.01	0.14	0.15	0.12	0.14
Oil ind. x post-09		−0.02	−0.02	−0.02	−0.02	−0.02

Note: Dependent variable is the number of any conflict events in the state in year t; all regressions include residuals from the first stage regressions of the endogenous price index on the excluded instruments as a control with appropriate standard errors (clustered at the state level) calculated; *, **, *** indicate statistical significance at the 10, 5, and 1 percent level, respectively. Data are for 37 states for 8 years (2004–11). All regressions include year and region-year effects and various controls (the log of population in 2003, the log of population density in 2003, the number of conflict events in 1997–2003, the poverty gap and headcount poverty in 2003, a dummy for multiple dominant ethnic groups, a dummy for more than 2 ethnic minorities, a dummy for whether the federal president is of the same ethnicity as the dominant group in the state, and the interaction between this variable and the multiple dominant groups dummy). The models are estimated through the population-averaged negative binomial estimator for panel data.

Table B.11 The Impact of Price Shocks on Conflict in Nigeria (2004–11), Robustness

	(1)	(2)	(3)	(4)	(5)
Method	Nbreg	Nbreg	Nbreg	Nbreg	Nbreg
Period	2004–10	2004–10	2004–11	2004–11	2004–11
Instruments	$CI_{NAR}^{oth}, PI_{NAR}^{oth}$	$CI_{NAR}^{oth}, PI_{NAR}^{oth}$	$CI_{NAR}^{oth}, PI_{NAR}^{oth}$		
$CI_{NAR}(t)$	0.024*	−0.021			
	(0.012)	(0.034)			
$PI_{NAR}(t)$	−0.010	0.035			
	(0.011)	(0.043)			
$CI_{NAR}(t-1)$		0.079	0.066**		
		(0.053)	(0.031)		
$PI_{NAR}(t-1)$		−0.049	−0.032		
		(0.070)	(0.054)		
$CI_{NAR}^{oth}(t-1)$				0.051***	
				(0.009)	
$PI_{NAR}^{oth}(t-1)$				0.015	
				(0.012)	
$CI_{NAR}^{Intl}(t-1)$					0.013*
					(0.008)
$PI_{NAR}^{Intl}(t-1)$					−0.001
					(0.024)
Oil ind. (t)	0.003***	0.001			
	(0.001)	(0.001)			
Oil ind. (t−1)		0.002***	0.003***	0.002***	0.002***
		(0.001)	(0.001)	(0.001)	(0.001)
Oil ind. (t) x post-09	−0.001				
	(0.001)				
Oil ind. (t−1) x post-09			−0.003***	−0.004***	−0.003***
			(0.001)	(0.001)	(0.001)
Controls	YES	YES	YES	YES	YES
Observations	259	259	296	296	296
CI + CI (t−1)		0.058**			
PI + PI (t−1)		−0.014			
Oil + Oil (t−1)		0.003***			

Note: Dependent variable is the number of any conflict events in the state in year t; all regressions include residuals from the first stage regressions of the endogenous price index on the excluded instruments as a control with appropriate standard errors (clustered at the state level) calculated; *, **, *** indicate statistical significance at the 10, 5, and 1 percent level, respectively. Data are for 37 states for 8 years (2004–11). All regressions include year and region-year effects. The models are estimated through the population-averaged negative binomial estimator for panel data.

and retrieve the respective estimated residual components of the price indices $\widehat{\mu_{srt}^{oth}}$ and $\widehat{v_{srt}^{oth}}$ or $\widehat{\mu_{srt}^{intl}}$ and $\widehat{v_{srt}^{intl}}$, which should contain the endogenous component of CI_{srt} (Cameron and Trivedi 2013) We then add these endogenous components of CI and PI to equation (B.4), which becomes (when using the domestic price indices of faraway states as instruments):

$$C_{srt} = \alpha_{rt} + \beta_1 CI_{st-1} + \beta_2 PI_{st-1} + \beta_3 P_{st-1}^{oil} + \beta_4 P_{st-1}^{oil} \times d_{2009} + AZ_s$$
$$+ BX_{st} + \widehat{\mu_{srt}^{oth}} + \widehat{v_{srt}^{oth}} + \varepsilon_{st} \tag{B.4'}$$

Table B.12 The Impact of Price Shocks on Various Types of Conflict in Nigeria (2004–11)

	(1)	(2)	(3)	(4)	(5)	(6)	(7)	(8)	(9)	(10)	(11)	(12)	(13)
	Events with fatalities			Battle events				Protests/riots		Violence against civilians			Fatalities
	CI_{NAR}^{oth} PI_{NAR}^{oth}	CI_{BR}^{oth} PI_{BR}^{oth}	CI_{NAR}^{Intl} PI_{NAR}^{Intl}	CI_{NAR}^{oth} PI_{NAR}^{oth}	CI_{BR}^{oth} PI_{BR}^{oth}	CI_{NAR}^{Intl} PI_{NAR}^{Intl}	CI_{NAR}^{oth} PI_{NAR}^{oth}	CI_{BR}^{oth} PI_{BR}^{oth}	CI_{NAR}^{Intl} PI_{NAR}^{Intl}	CI_{NAR}^{oth} PI_{NAR}^{oth}	CI_{BR}^{oth} PI_{BR}^{oth}	CI_{NAR}^{Intl} PI_{NAR}^{Intl}	CI_{NAR}^{oth} PI_{NAR}^{oth}
$CI_{NAR}(t-1)$	0.059***		0.063*	0.054***		0.017	0.080		-0.002	0.038**		0.033	0.068***
	(0.016)		(0.033)	(0.015)		(0.034)	(0.058)		(0.041)	(0.016)		(0.032)	(0.013)
$PI_{NAR}(t-1)$	-0.027**		0.008	-0.043***		0.012	-0.025		0.029	-0.034**		-0.020	-0.021**
	(0.011)		(0.023)	(0.014)		(0.028)	(0.107)		(0.026)	(0.014)		(0.024)	(0.009)
$CI_{BR}(t-1)$		0.042***			0.044***			0.040***			0.029**		
		(0.014)			(0.012)			(0.014)			(0.014)		
$PI_{BR}(t-1)$		-0.014			-0.036**			-0.032**			-0.027**		
		(0.012)			(0.012)			(0.014)			(0.012)		
Oil ind. $(t-1)$	0.003***	0.003***	0.003***	0.004***	0.003*	0.003***	0.000	0.000	-0.001*	0.003***	0.003***	0.003***	0.001*
	(0.001)	(0.001)	(0.001)	(0.001)	(0.001)	(0.001)	(0.001)	(0.001)	(0.001)	(0.001)	(0.001)	(0.001)	(0.001)
Oil ind. (t) x post-09	-0.004***	-0.004***	-0.004***	-0.004**	-0.004***	-0.004***	-0.003	-0.003	-0.003*	-0.002**	-0.002**	-0.002***	-0.006***
	(0.001)	(0.001)	(0.001)	(0.002)	(0.002)	(0.002)	(0.002)	(0.002)	(0.002)	(0.001)	(0.001)	(0.001)	(0.001)

Note: All regressions include residuals from the first stage regressions of the endogenous price index on the excluded instruments as a control with appropriate standard errors (clustered at the state level) calculated; *, **, *** indicate statistical significance at the 10, 5, and 1 percent level, respectively. Data are for 37 states for 8 years (2004–11). All regressions include year and region-year effects, and a full set of controls as in tables B.10 and B.11. The models are estimated through the population-averaged negative binomial estimator for panel data.

Table B.13 Mediating Factors Affecting the Impact of Price Shocks on Conflict

	Any events	Events with fat.	Battles	Protests and riots	civ. violence
election x CI (t−1)	0.034**	0.034**	0.030*	−0.003	0.030**
election x PI (t−1)	−0.023	−0.036**	0.010	−0.024	−0.049***
election x Oil Ind (t−1)	0.002***	0.002	0.001	0.002	0.002**
cost_lagos x CI (t−1)	−0.000	0.000	−0.001	−0.001**	−0.000
cost_lagos x PI (t−1)	0.001**	0.000	0.001**	−0.001**	0.001
president x CI (t−1)	−0.001	−0.019	−0.018	0.006	0.020
president x PI (t−1)	−0.002	0.008	0.009	−0.015	−0.013
president x Oil Ind (t−1)	−0.002	−0.000	−0.003***	0.002*	−0.001
unem03 x CI (t−1)	−0.000	−0.001	−0.001	−0.000	−0.000
unem03 x PI (t−1)	0.001	0.001	0.001	0.001	0.001
unem03 x Oil Ind (t−1)	−0.000	−0.000	−0.000	0.000**	−0.000
mult_domin x CI (t−1)	−0.016	0.022	0.003	−0.002	−0.006
mult_domin x PI (t−1)	−0.008	−0.035**	−0.039	−0.015	−0.015
mult_domin x Oil Ind (t−1)	0.003***	0.002**	0.004***	0.001	0.003***
many_minor x CI (t−1)	−0.011	0.029	−0.002	−0.045	0.009
many_minor x PI (t−1)	0.007	−0.027	−0.000	0.022	−0.000
many_minor x Oil Ind (t−1)	0.004***	0.002***	0.005***	0.001	0.004***
pov03 x CI (t−1)	0.000	−0.000	−0.000	0.000	0.000
pov03 x PI (t−1)	−0.000	0.000	−0.000	−0.000	−0.000
pov03 x Oil Ind (t−1)	−0.000	−0.000	−0.000	−0.000	−0.000
gini03 x CI (t−1)	−0.270**	−0.223	−0.187	−0.072	−0.708***
gini03 x PI (t−1)	0.256*	0.270	0.184	0.070	0.729***
gini03 x Oil Ind (t−1)	0.038***	0.046***	0.063***	0.002	0.030***
Past conflict x CI (t−1)	−0.000	−0.000	−0.001**	0.002*	−0.001
Past conflict x PI (t−1)	−0.000	−0.000	0.001*	−0.003**	0.001
Past conflict x Oil ind (t−1)	−0.000	−0.000	−0.000	−0.000***	0.000

Note: The table reports the coefficients of the interaction terms between the price indices and various conditioning factors obtained from different regressions; all regressions include residuals from the first stage regressions of the endogenous price index on the excluded instruments as a control with appropriate standard errors (clustered at the state level) calculated; *, **, *** indicate statistical significance at the 10, 5, and 1 percent level, respectively (based on adjusted standard errors). Data are for 37 states for 8 years (2004–11). All regressions include year and region-year effects and a full set of controls as in tables B.10 and B.11. The models are estimated through the population-averaged negative binomial estimator for panel data.

The coefficients of CI and PI should not suffer from endogeneity bias as the residuals from the first stage should purge the endogenous component of the price indices. This formulation ensures the computation of consistent standard errors (Cameron and Trivedi 2013). The signs of the residuals (not reported in the tables but available upon request) confirm the direction of the endogeneity bias, that is negative for CI and positive for PI. In other words, by reducing the

Table B.14 The Impact of Changes in Trade Prices on the Boko Haram Conflict (2010–13)

	(1)	(2)	(3)	(4)	(5)	(6)	(7)	(8)
Region	All	North	All	North	North	North	North	North
Dep. variable	BH event	BH event	Non BH event	Non BH event	BH fat. event	Non BH fat. event	BH fatalities	Non BH fatalities
$CI^{Intl}_{NAR}(t-1)$	0.046**	0.067***	−0.013	0.014	0.116***	0.010	0.078***	−0.025
	(0.020)	(0.018)	(0.011)	(0.013)	(0.018)	(0.016)	(0.024)	(0.022)
$PI^{Intl}_{NAR}(t-1)$	−0.105**	−0.093**	−0.003	0.008	−0.024	−0.000	0.020	0.050
	(0.043)	(0.043)	(0.018)	(0.023)	(0.026)	(0.023)	(0.038)	(0.034)
Oil ind. $(t-1)$	0.001		−0.001***					
	(0.002)		(0.000)					
Observations	148	80	148	80	80	80	80	80
Nr. of states	37	20	37	20	20	20	20	20

Note: Robust standard errors in parentheses; *, **, *** indicate statistical significance at the 10, 5, and 1 percent level, respectively. All regressions include year and region-year effects and a full set of controls as in in tables B.10 and B.11. The models are estimated through the population-averaged negative binomial estimator for panel data.

demand for products, conflict reduces the prices of consumed goods and thus it generates a spurious negative correlation between CI and conflict. The opposite is true for PI. Therefore in both cases the endogeneity biases the CI and PI coefficient toward zero.

As it turns out, the international price indices have a weak predictive power for *CI* and *PI* because of the different composition of the items' basket and the limited transmission of international commodity prices to the Nigerian market. However, the international price indices are useful, since (unlike the domestic price indices) they are available through 2013.

These results are robust to using the instrumented PI and CI constructed through the broad matching of the items (column 4). However, the results for production are not robust to using the PI instrumented through the international prices whether through the narrow (column 5) or the broad matching (column 6). On the other hand, the result for CI holds although the coefficient is less significant. These weaker results suggest that the two problems described above (limited transmission of international to domestic prices and limited number of items matched) in using international prices to capture price shocks at the local level may be important in the case of Nigeria.[9] The oil index coefficients are unaffected by the use of international prices for CI and PI.

Israeli-Palestinian conflict

We estimate the following equation using a Negative Binomial regression, which is an appropriate method for analyzing count data characterized by many zeros and by over-dispersion (Long and Freese 2006):

$$F_{lr} = \gamma_r + \beta_1 \Delta EXP_l + BX_l + \varepsilon_l, \tag{B.9}$$

where *F* is the number of fatalities in each locality *l* in region *r* during the period of September 2000 and December 2004. The change in Palestinian exports in each locality, ΔEXP_l, is calculated as the sum of the change in exports in each sector s during the 1996–99 period weighted by the share of employment in that sector in the locality's total private employment in 1997[10]:

$$\Delta EXP_l = \sum_{s=1}^{N} \left(\Delta exp_s \times \frac{emp_{ls}^{1997}}{emp_{l}^{1997}} \right) \tag{B.10}$$

This measure of exposure to the export changes is close in spirit to Topalova (2010) and should capture the effect of exports on conflict via employment. Thus it should provide for a direct test of the opportunity cost hypothesis. An appealing feature of this measure for our identification is that it should be exogenous to changes in local conditions related to conflict. We provide below evidence in support of this exogeneity hypothesis by showing that the ΔEXP coefficient is not affected when instrumenting ΔEXP through measures using plausibly exogenous sources of export changes.

The specification (B.9) includes also region effects (where the regions are Gaza Strip, Jerusalem, and the West Bank) as well as the vector X, which contains a host of sociodemographic variables at the locality level that might affect the distribution of employment across sectors and the level of conflict. These variables refer to 1997 and include the total population, share of males in the population, share of the population aged 15–40, share of population with elementary education or below, share of households with more than 8 members, and the share of married individuals. We also control for other factors that may foster Palestinian grievances. First, we include controls for the availability of public utilities such as water, electricity, sewage, and landline telephones. Second, we control for the unemployment rate in 1997 (computed from the census). Third, we also control for the number of permits to work in Israel in 1999, which Miaari, Zussman, and Zussman (2014) show to be associated with the subsequent violence. Finally, to control for the cyclicality of the conflict, the vector X includes also the number of Palestinian fatalities in each locality between January 1995 and August 2000. The error term is ε and standard errors are robust.

In some specifications, we also account for other local labor market characteristics that might be correlated with changes in exports as well as violence. These controls include the locality-wise distribution of Palestinian workers across the main types of employment (i.e. private and public sector and Israel), their relative wages in 1999 (i.e. the first year these data are available from the PLFS), and the distribution across location types, i.e. urban, rural, or refugee camp.

In some specifications, we split the change in total Palestinian exports into exports to Israel, the dominant export market, and exports to the rest of the world, both weighted according to equation (B.10). We also test for the effects of changes in Palestinian imports between 1996 and 1999, ΔIMP, weighted by the employment shares as described in equation (B.10):

$$F_{lr} = \gamma_r + \beta_1 \Delta EXP_l + \beta_2 \Delta IMP_l + BX_l + \varepsilon_l \tag{B.11}$$

We also estimate an alternative model to investigate whether changes in Palestinian exports affect the probability of violence in different localities. In order to do this, instead of using the number of fatalities in each locality we construct an indicator variable that equals 1 if the locality experienced a positive number of fatalities during the Second Intifada and zero otherwise.[11] We estimate this specification using a probit model.

In order to substantiate the argument that the trade measures are exogenous to local level conditions related to the conflict, we also instrument the export (and other import) measures. In order to do so we use instruments based on plausibly exogenous sources of Palestinian export changes. In particular we use two such sources. The first is the changes in Chinese export supply over the same period (1996–99). This is arguably an important source of competition of Palestinian exports especially in Israel. Indeed, unlike imports from the West Bank and Gaza, Israeli imports from China dramatically increased between 1995 and 2000 (figure 1.13). In order to ensure the exogeneity of Chinese exports changes to Israeli conditions (which may be related to the conflict prospects), we take the changes in Chinese sectoral exports to the world but Israel. We replace the Palestinian exports with this variable in equation (B.10) to generate the first instrument ($\Delta ChnExp$). A rise in Chinese sectoral exports may also be related to a general increase in the world demand in those sectors. To control for this effect we also add an instrument, which is constructed again as in equation (B.10) but using world sectoral exports instead of Palestinian exports ($\Delta WldExp$).

The second source of exogenous changes in Palestinian exports is Israeli trade policy. In particular Israel, as much of the rest of the world, undertook a substantial process of (unilateral) tariff liberalization during the 1990s, which reduced import duties in most sectors. The scale of this reduction can be gauged in figure B.1, which reports the distribution of the nonzero Most

Figure B.1 Changes in Israeli MFN Tariffs (5-digit SITC Rev. 3), 1993–2004

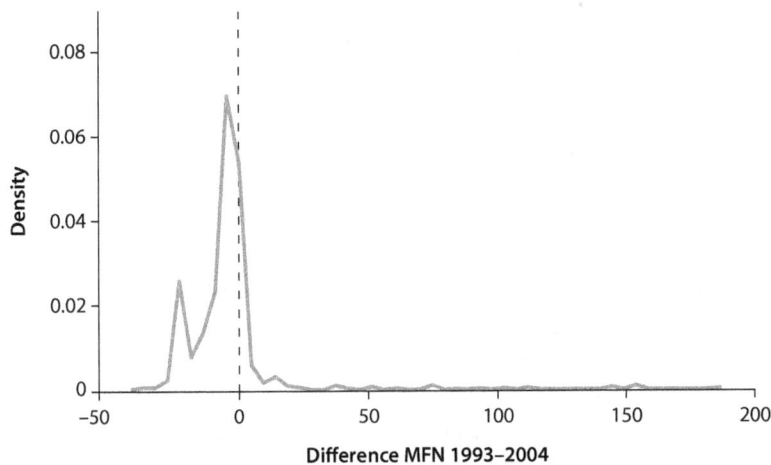

Source: WITS.

Favoured Nation (MFN) tariff differences between 1993 and 2004 (the only years during that period for which data are available in WITS). This reduction in Israeli tariffs caused a reduction in the preferential access of Palestinian exports to their major destination market, thus effectively acting as a reduction in demand for Palestinian goods from Israel.[12] Again we use the change in Israeli tariffs to replace the changes in Palestinian exports in equation (B.10) to generate the instrument for ΔEXP (i.e. $\Delta IsrMFN$).[13] The main problem with this instrument is that it covers a larger period of time than do the changes in pre-Intifada trade that we are considering. Because of that we also check the robustness of the results to excluding this instrument from the first stage estimation.

We instrument the ΔEXP with this series of variables in the following first stage specification:

$$\Delta EXP_{lr} = \gamma_r + \alpha_1 \Delta ChnExp_l + \alpha_2 \Delta WldExp_l + \alpha_3 \Delta IsrMFN_l + BX_l + \mu_l \quad \text{(B.12)}$$

The results of this specification—presented in table B.21—suggest that these instruments are good predictors of changes in Palestinian exports over 1996–99. In particular $\Delta ChnExp$ is negatively associated with Palestinian export changes in line with the idea that Chinese exports may displace Palestinian exports. Conversely the coefficient of $\Delta WldExp$ is positive and significant as world demand positively affects Palestinian exports as well. Similarly, $\Delta IsrMFN$ has a positive and significant coefficient consistent with the hypothesis that a reduction in Israeli import tariffs to the rest of the world induces also a reduction in Palestinian exports (as competition in the Israeli market increases). These instruments appear to be relevant also in explaining Palestinian exports to Israel and to the rest of the world. It is noticeable that the effect of Israeli tariffs is of opposite sign in the case of Palestinian exports to the rest of the world than in the case of Palestinian exports to Israel (column 5). This suggests a reorientation of Palestinian exports away from the Israeli market as a result of a reduction in preferential access to Israel.

We follow a similar procedure to that of the Nigerian analysis to correct for the endogeneity bias on the basis of this first stage. Armed with the estimated endogenous component of ΔEXP computed from equation (B.12), we add that in equation (B.9), which becomes:

$$F_{lt} = \gamma_r + b_1 \Delta EXP + BX_l + \widehat{\mu}_l + \varepsilon_l \quad \text{(B.9')}$$

Table B.19 presents the results of this equation, which confirm the robustness of the effects of changes in Palestinian exports on subsequent conflict intensity. The b_1 coefficient is slightly larger in absolute term than the comparable coefficient in table B.15. That is especially when excluding $\Delta IsrMFN$ from the instrument set (column 2). However, the magnitude of the coefficient is not statistically different from that in table B.15, thus confirming that the endogeneity bias is limited in this context. The results also hold for Palestinian

Table B.15 The Impact of Palestinian Exports on Conflict Intensity

	(1)	(2)	(3)	(4)	(5)	(6)
Region	All	All	All	All	West Bank	Gaza
Sample	All	All	LFS	LFS	All	All
ΔPalestinian exports$_{96-99}$	−0.125***	−0.128***	−0.137***	−0.159***	−0.086***	−0.528*
	(0.029)	(0.030)	(0.051)	(0.050)	(0.028)	(0.283)
Population	0.000*	0.000	0.000	0.000	0.000*	0.000
Male share	−5.701	−5.959	−10.663	−4.296	−5.143	−84.722
Age 15–40	−0.739	−0.123	9.395	14.063*	−0.034	−85.317*
Education	−1.917*	−1.865*	−1.491	−3.292*	−2.047*	−16.864*
Share refugees	0.209	0.276	−0.215	0.501	0.110	2.173*
Large households (%)	−3.845***	−4.017***	−3.301*	−3.489*	−3.352***	7.556
Married (%)	−12.299***	−12.242***	−22.521***	−22.195***	−12.432***	−2.373
Gaza	0.272	0.100	−0.332	−0.059		
Jerusalem	0.165	0.140	−0.473	−0.956**	0.330	
Public water	0.167	0.162	−0.269	−0.183	−0.049	−0.603
Public electricity	0.113	0.095	−0.300	−0.215	0.428	−6.386***
Public sewage	1.329***	1.339***	0.326	1.049***	1.146***	0.836
Telephone lines	1.290***	1.285***	1.323***	1.501***	1.084***	4.026*
Work permits to Israel		0.001	0.002***	0.002***	0.002	0.001**
Past Pal. Fatalities		−0.021	0.076**	0.059	−0.198***	−0.001
Unemployment		0.275	−0.823	−1.356	0.694	−1.645
Empl. Israel (%)			−0.015			
Avg. wage emp. Israel			0.018**			
Empl. Public (%)			0.065			
Avg. wage emp. Public			−0.009			
Private empl. (%)			0.038			
Avg. wage emp. Private			−0.013**			
Urban (%)			1.179***			
Refugee camp (%)			1.535***			
Observations	569	569	199	199	532	37
Marginal effect ΔEXP	−0.091	−0.092	−0.312	−0.430	−0.049	−0.691

Note: The dependent variable is the number of fatalities from politically motivated violence (Palestinians killed by Israelis) from the outbreak of the Second Intifada (September 28, 2000) until December 2004 in locality. See table A.7 for the definitions of the independent variables. The regressions are estimated using a Negative Binomial model. Robust standard errors (clustered at the locality level) are reported in parentheses. The symbols *, **, *** represent statistical significance at the 10, 5, and 1 percent levels.

exports to Israel (columns 3–4), while they are weaker for Palestinian exports to the rest of the world, probably due to the relatively weak power of the instruments in predicting this variable.

The results are also robust to including the predicted import variables using the same instrument set (columns 5–7). These variables continue to be not significant even in these specifications.[14] The b_1 coefficient is also robust to using the restricted LFS sample (column 8) and it is also robust when considering the 532 localities in the West Bank (columns 9–10). On the other hand, it

Table B.16 The Impact of Palestinian Trade on Conflict Intensity

Sample	(1) All	(2) All	(3) All	(4) LFS	(5) All	(6) All	(7) LFS
ΔPalestinian exports$_{96-99}$	-0.121***	-0.127***	-0.122***	-0.146***			
	(0.029)	(0.030)	(0.029)	(0.052)			
ΔPalestinian exports to Israel$_{96-99}$					-0.147***	-0.133***	-0.120
					(0.041)	(0.042)	(0.075)
ΔPalestinian exports to RoW$_{96-99}$					-0.231	-0.179	-0.028
					(0.162)	(0.175)	(0.302)
ΔPalestinian imports$_{96-99}$	-0.006		-0.004	-0.016		-0.004	-0.017
	(0.005)		(0.008)	(0.012)		(0.008)	(0.012)
ΔIsraeli imports from RoW$_{96-99}$		0.003	0.001	-0.005		0.001	-0.005
		(0.003)	(0.004)	(0.004)		(0.005)	(0.004)
Other controls	YES	YES	YES	YES	YES	YES	YES
Observations	569	569	569	199	569	569	199

Notes: The dependent variable is the number of fatalities from politically motivated violence (Palestinians killed by Israelis) from the outbreak of the Second Intifada (September 28, 2000) until December 2004 in locality. See table A.7 for the definitions of the independent variables. Other controls include all the controls in table B.15 column 2. The regressions are estimated using a Negative Binomial model. Robust standard errors (clustered at the locality level) are reported in parentheses. The symbols *, **, *** represent statistical significance at the 10, 5, and 1 percent levels.

Table B.17 The Impact of Palestinian Trade on a Different Measure of Conflict Intensity

Dep. variable	(1)	(2)	(3)	(4)
	Palestinian fatalities during hostilities and demonstrations			
ΔPalestinian exports$_{96-99}$	−0.150***	−0.137***		
	(0.041)	(0.042)		
ΔPalestinian exports to Israel$_{96-99}$			−0.187***	−0.175***
			(0.050)	(0.051)
ΔPalestinian exports to RoW$_{96-99}$			−0.355*	−0.340
			(0.213)	(0.218)
ΔPalestinian imports$_{96-99}$		−0.012		−0.011
		(0.009)		(0.009)
ΔIsraeli imports from RoW$_{96-99}$		−0.003		−0.004
		(0.005)		(0.005)
Other controls	YES	YES	YES	YES
Observations	569	569	569	569

Notes: The dependent variable is the number of fatalities from politically motivated violence during demonstration (Palestinians killed by Israelis) from the outbreak of the Second Intifada (September 28, 2000) until December 2004 in locality. See table A.7 for the definitions of the independent variables. Other controls include all the controls in table B.17, column 2. The regressions are estimated using a Negative Binomial model. Robust standard errors (clustered at the locality level) are reported in parentheses. The symbols *, **, *** represent statistical significance at the 10, 5, and 1 percent levels.

Table B.18 The Impact of Palestinian Trade on Conflict Probability

Dep. variable	(1)	(2)	(3)	(4)
	Dummy at least 1 fatality			
ΔPalestinian exports$_{96-99}$	−0.053***	−0.055***		
	(0.017)	(0.018)		
ΔPalestinian exports to Israel$_{96-99}$			−0.063**	−0.069***
			(0.025)	(0.026)
ΔPalestinian exports to RoW$_{96-99}$			−0.107	−0.131
			(0.103)	(0.105)
ΔPalestinian imports$_{96-99}$		0.002		0.002
		(0.006)		(0.006)
ΔIsraeli imports from RoW$_{96-99}$		−0.000		−0.001
		(0.003)		(0.003)
Other controls	YES	YES	YES	YES
Observations	569	569	569	569

Notes: The dependent variable is a dummy for whether the locality experienced at least one fatality from politically motivated violence (Palestinians killed by Israelis) from the outbreak of the Second Intifada (September 28, 2000) until December 2004. See table A.7 for the definitions of the independent variables. Other controls include all the controls in table B.15, column 2. The regressions are estimated using a probit model. Robust standard errors (clustered at the locality level) are reported in parentheses. The symbols *, **, *** represent statistical significance at the 10, 5, and 1 percent levels.

is not robust for the 37 localities in Gaza (columns 11–12). Finally, the results also hold for fatalities as a result of hostilities or demonstrations (column 13) as well as for conflict probability (column 14). The instrumentation again slightly raises the effect of changes in exports on the latter: a USD 10 million increase in export in a sector which employs 10 percent of private employees in a locality is associated with a reduction in the probability of conflict in that locality by 7.8 percent.

Table B.19 The Impact of Palestinian Trade on Conflict: Tackling Endogeneity

Dep. Variable	(1)	(2)	(3)	(4)	(5)	(6)	(7)
	Palestinian fatalities during the 2nd Intifada						
ΔPalestinian exp$_{96-99}$	−0.161*** (0.036)	−0.174*** (0.037)			−0.144*** (0.044)	−0.169*** (0.036)	−0.164*** (0.051)
ΔPalestinian exp. to Israel$_{96-99}$			−0.161*** (0.053)	−0.136** (0.057)			
ΔPalestinian exp. to RoW$_{96-99}$			−0.175 (0.216)	0.053 (0.271)			
ΔPalestinian imports$_{96-99}$					0.024 (0.034)		0.000 (0.041)
ΔIsraeli imp. from RoW$_{96-99}$						0.008 (0.007)	0.006 (0.009)
Instruments	All	ΔChnExp ΔWldExp	All	ΔChnExp ΔWldExp	All	All	All
Observations	569	569	569	569	569	569	569

	(8)	(9)	(10)	(11)	(12)	(13)	(14)
Sample	LFS	All	All	All	All	All	All
Region	All	West Bank	West Bank	Gaza	Gaza	All	All
Dep. Variable	*Palestinian fatalities during the 2nd Intifada*					Fat demo	Dummy
ΔPalestinian exp.$_{96-99}$	−0.190** (0.071)	−0.124*** (0.034)		−0.169 (0.356)		−0.139*** (0.052)	−0.082*** (0.024)
ΔPalestinian exp. to Israel$_{96-99}$			−0.131*** (0.046)		1.969 (1.281)		
ΔPalestinian exp. to RoW$_{96-99}$			−0.173 (0.195)		8.067 (4.995)		
Instruments	All	All	All	All	All	All	All
Observations	199	532	532	37	37	569	569

Note: The regressions are estimated using a Negative Binomial model except column 14 which is estimated through a probit model. See table A.7 for the definitions of the independent variables. Other controls include all the controls in table B.15, column 2. All regressions include the estimated residual term of the first stage (table B.23). Robust standard errors (clustered at the locality level) are reported in parentheses. The symbols *, **, *** represent statistical significance at the 10, 5, and 1 percent levels.

Table B.20 The Heterogeneity of the Impact of Export Changes on Conflict Intensity

Dep. variable	(1)	(2)	(3)	(4)	(5)	(6)	(7)	(8)
	Palestinian fatalities during the 2nd Intifada							
Pre-Intifada Fatal. x ΔPalExp	0.003 (0.032)							0.004 (0.034)
Refugee (%) x ΔPalExp		−0.204** (0.087)						−0.214** (0.094)
Male (%) x ΔPalExp			1.696*** (0.589)					1.681*** (0.603)
Large HH (%) x ΔPalExp				−0.162 (0.192)				−0.166 (0.222)
Unemployment (%) x ΔPalExp					−0.426* (0.245)			−0.158 (0.273)

table continues next page

Table B.20 The Heterogeneity of the Impact of Export Changes on Conflict Intensity (continued)

	(1)	(2)	(3)	(4)	(5)	(6)	(7)	(8)
Dep. variable				Palestinian fatalities during the 2nd Intifada				
Age 15–40 (%) x ΔPalExp						0.359		0.623
						(0.487)		(0.634)
Educated (%) x ΔPalExp							0.119	0.251
							(0.164)	(0.176)
Other controls	YES	YES	YES	YES	YES	YES	YES	YES
Observations	569	569	569	569	569	569	569	569

Notes: The dependent variable is the number of fatalities from politically motivated violence during demonstration (Palestinians killed by Israelis) from the outbreak of the Second Intifada (September 28, 2000) until December 2004 in locality. See table A.7 for the definitions of the independent variables. Other controls include ΔPalestinian exports$_{1996-99}$ and all the controls in table B.15, column 2. The regressions are estimated using a Negative Binomial model. Robust standard errors (clustered at the locality level) are reported in parentheses. The symbols *, **, *** represent statistical significance at the 10, 5, and 1 percent levels.

Table B.21 Instrumenting Palestinian Exports through Exogenous Shocks

	(1)	(2)	(3)	(4)	(5)	(6)
Dep. variable	ΔPalestinian exports$_{96-99}$		ΔPalestinian exports to Israel$_{96-99}$		ΔPalestinian exports to RoW$_{96-99}$	
ΔChinese exports to the world but Israel	−0.002***	−0.006***	−0.002***	−0.007***	−0.000**	0.002***
	(0.001)	(0.000)	(0.001)	(0.001)	(0.000)	(0.000)
ΔWorld exports	0.001***	0.001***	0.001***	0.001***	−0.000***	0.000
	(0.000)	(0.000)	(0.000)	(0.000)	(0.000)	(0.000)
ΔMFN tariff	0.801***		1.303***		−0.502***	
	(0.130)		(0.155)		(0.034)	
Other controls	YES	YES	YES	YES	YES	YES
Observations	569	569	569	569	569	569
R-squared	0.557	0.501	0.585	0.492	0.687	0.445

Note: The regressions are estimated using an OLS model. Robust standard errors (clustered at the locality level) are reported in parentheses. The symbols *, **, *** represent statistical significance at the 10, 5, and 1 percent levels. Other controls include all the controls in table B.15, column 2.

Notes

1. This means that conflict onset is coded as zero in the nonconflict years, 1 in the first year of conflict and missing in the following years of conflict. This is a departure from much of the previous literature, which uses a dummy for the first year of conflict (and zero otherwise) to measure conflict onset. Ending would take the value of zero during the conflict; the value of 1 in the first year of peace and missing in the other years.

2. In particular Bazzi and Blattman (2014) and Bruckner and Ciccone (2010) use $j \in [0; 2]$.

3. King and Zeng (2001) define "rare events" dependent variables as those for which the number of zeros are larger than that of ones by at least an order of magnitude in the dozens.

4. King and Zeng (2001) also propose a rare logit estimator to correct the rare event bias. Unfortunately the lack of convergence in the estimation of our model does not allow us to implement that estimator.

5. Within the negative binomial model option in STATA, we use the population-averaged (PA) option that relaxes the assumption of independence of C_{srt} to allow

for different correlations over time of the conflict. The relaxation of this assumption is useful for the purpose of our analysis, given that conflict in 2001 may not be correlated with conflict in 2003 and 2010 the same way. The other two options, random effect (RE) and fixed effect (FE), are attractive but do not adequately capture our data and impose additional structure on the data that cannot be validated. Also, they attempt to model over-dispersion rather than capturing fixed effects at the state level and may have convergence issues given the size of our data.

6. We also tried a dummy for whether the state has more than one dominant ethnic group, but its effect was never significant in explaining conflict.

7. In addition, an inspection of the consumption and production data from the household survey suggests that none of the states is large enough to substantially influence the prices of the top-produced and -consumed commodities across the entire country. This adds confidence to the claim of exogeneity of this instrument.

8. The results do not change without weights. We also experiment with different distance thresholds, i.e. 3, 4, 6, and 7 hours obtaining similar results (results available upon request).

9. Indeed, in parallel preliminary work we document the limited pass-through from international to domestic prices in Nigeria for various agricultural items.

10. Note that all the results are robust to computing the changes over the 1997–1999 period or the 1996–2000 period (results available upon request).

11. This variable is also identical to an indicator variable that equals 1 if the number of fatalities in the locality is above or equal to the median number of fatalities across localities and zero otherwise.

12. As a de facto customs union, Palestinian and Israeli goods do not pay any duties to access the reciprocal markets.

13. Unlike trade data, we cannot sum tariff rates over the sectors to match the 5-digit SITC level data of MFN tariff with the 2-digit ISIC employment data. Instead we take the average of tariff rates across 5-digit SITC sectors weighted by Palestinian total exports in each sector. In this way we ensure that the changes in Israeli tariffs are weighted by the importance they may have for Palestinian sectoral exports.

14. The results are also robust to including the non instrumented import variables (results available upon request).

References

Alesina, A., A. Devleeschauwer, R. Wacziarg, S. Kurlat, and W. Easterly. 2003. "Fractionalization." *Journal of Economic Growth* 8 (2): 155–94.

Bazzi, S., and C. Blattman. 2014. "Economic Shocks and Conflict: Evidence from Commodity Prices." *American Economic Journal: Macroeconomics*.

Beck, N., and J. Katz. 2011. "Modeling Dynamics in Time-Series-Cross-Section Political Economy Data." *Annual Review of Political Science* 14: 331–52.

Bruckner, M., and A. Ciccone. 2010. "International Commodity Prices, Growth and the Outbreak of Civil War in Sub-Saharan Africa." *The Economic Journal* 120 (May): 519–34.

Cameron, C., and P. K. Trivedi. 2013. *Regression Analysis of Count Data.* Cambridge, UK: Cambridge University Press.

Chaudion, S., Z. Peskowitz, and C. Stanton. 2012. "Beyond Zeroes and Ones: The Effect of Income on the Severity and Evolution of Civil Conflict." Mimeo.

Dube, O., and J. Vargas. 2013. "Commodity Price Shocks and Civil Conflict: Evidence from Colombia." *Review of Economic Studies* 80 (4): 1384–421.

Jacoby, H. 2013. "Food Prices, Wages, and Welfare in Rural India." Policy Research Working Paper 6412, World Bank.

King, G., and L. Zeng. 2001. "Logistic Regression in Rare Events Data." *Political Analysis* 9: 137–63.

Kuhn, P., and N. Weidmann. 2013. "Unequal We Fight: Between- and Within-Group Inequality and Ethnic Civil War." Princeton University, Mimeo.

Long, J. S., and J. Freese. 2006. *Regression Models for Categorical Dependent Variables Using Stata.* 2nd ed. College Station, TX: Stata Press.

Miaari, S., A. Zussman, and N. Zussman. 2014. "Employment Restrictions and Political Violence in the Israeli-Palestinian Conflict." *Journal of Economic Behavior and Organization* 101 (May): 24–44.

Montalvo, J. G., and M. Reynal-Querol. 2005. "Ethnic Polarization, Potential Conflict, and Civil Wars." *American Economic Review* 95 (3).

Powell, J. M., and C. L. Thyne. 2011. "Global Instances of Coups from 1950 to 2010: A New Dataset." *Journal of Peace Research* 48 (2): 249–59.

Topalova, P. 2010. "Factor Immobility and Regional Impacts of Trade Liberalization: Evidence on Poverty from India." *American Economic Journal: Applied Economics* 2: 1–41.

World Bank. 2011. *World Development Report 2011: Conflict, Security and Development.* Washington, DC: World Bank.

Environmental Benefits Statement

The World Bank Group is committed to reducing its environmental footprint. In support of this commitment, the Publishing and Knowledge Division leverages electronic publishing options and print-on-demand technology, which is located in regional hubs worldwide. Together, these initiatives enable print runs to be lowered and shipping distances decreased, resulting in reduced paper consumption, chemical use, greenhouse gas emissions, and waste.

The Publishing and Knowledge Division follows the recommended standards for paper use set by the Green Press Initiative. Whenever possible, books are printed on 50 percent to 100 percent postconsumer recycled paper, and at least 50 percent of the fiber in our book paper is either unbleached or bleached using Totally Chlorine Free (TCF), Processed Chlorine Free (PCF), or Enhanced Elemental Chlorine Free (EECF) processes.

More information about the Bank's environmental philosophy can be found at http://crinfo.worldbank.org/wbcrinfo/node/4.

green
press
INITIATIVE

www.ingramcontent.com/pod-product-compliance
Lightning Source LLC
Chambersburg PA
CBHW082357270326
41935CB00013B/1662